HUBSPOT CRM

SIMPLIFIED

Win more customers, grow your business and make more money with HubSpot CRM

Ramanathan J

Cover designed by Ramanathan J

Table of Contents

INTRODUCTION

What is the most important objective for any business owner or the head of a marketing function in any organization? The answer is to grow the business by generating more revenue from sales. This answer may seem simple and obvious but we can find many companies in the market who struggle to achieve this objective. Why does increasing the growth seem to be an arduous task for many businesses? Increased competition is indeed one of the crucial factors when it comes to determining the business growth for any company. However, business owners or decision makers must consider another important aspect for revenue generation and that is to store and to access customer and prospect data in an efficient and effective manner.

Customer data that is managed in a coherent style can provide a decisive competitive edge to the marketing and sales strategies of organizations. Customer Relationship Management or CRM software products help companies to store their customer related data. Some of the most popular CRM software products include Zoho CRM and Salesforce and HubSpot.

This book will focus upon HubSpot CRM. HubSpot offers a free version of the CRM product to any user who signs up. Businesses can start using the free version of HubSpot CRM to manage their customer and account related data. Business owners can use the free HubSpot CRM to organize, track and to build better relationships with their leads and customers.

Apart from the free CRM software, HubSpot also offers additional products such as Marketing Hub, Sales Hub, Service Hub and HubSpot CMS. As your business expands, you can purchase the Starter, Professional or Enterprise versions of Marketing, Sales or Service Hubs that will meet your additional business requirements.

Need for CRM:

A business owner may wonder as to why he/she needs a CRM software and how this product would add value to his/her company.

Now if you are running a small business or a company, then you can manually track your interactions with the few customers who do business with you. However, when your business will scale, it will become difficult for your company to manually track all the interactions that are happening with every customer. Hence, you can invest in a CRM system that can enable your business to scale in future.

A CRM system can empower salespersons to understand if any other sales associate has already contacted a prospect and if so, what were the topics that were covered in the call. A CRM system stores all the information related to interaction between sales associates and a prospect. CRM system improves communication between the sales team and various prospects.

A CRM can provide an accurate record of prospect history in a couple of clicks. A CRM can also standardize how sales associates track activities with various prospects. As a result, managers can handle their teams in a better manner.

Hence, a CRM system can provide a governance mechanism for sales processes in organizations. Businesses can transition from handling their interactions with leads or prospects in an ad-hoc manner to managing the engagements of various sales associates with prospects in a systematic manner.

HubSpot CRM can provide you with a free platform to organize, track and nurture your relationships with leads and customers. Other premium products such as Marketing Hub can enable companies to grow traffic to their websites. Similarly, Sales Hub can help businesses to extract deeper insights about their prospects. Sales Hub can help companies to automate repetitive tasks thereby closing deals quickly.

GETTING STARTED

We will now look at the initial steps that we have to complete before we can use HubSpot CRM to manage customer and prospect data. We will consider a case study or a sample organization for whom we will be using HubSpot CRM to manage current customer and new prospect data.

Case Study:

Let us assume that we are running a yoga studio business in Miami, USA. We will call our yoga studio business as MiamiYoga. The yoga studio business has two properties near the South beach where customers come to attend Yoga sessions. These customers can enroll for daily Yoga sessions or for weekends only Yoga sessions.

Yoga sessions are clubbed into monthly, quarterly, half-yearly or annual programs and customers can enroll for any of these programs.

MiamiYoga has a fleet of instructors who train and guide customers during Yoga sessions. MiamiYoga now plans to start a corporate wellness program in which companies can partner with MiamiYoga to provide Yoga based wellness benefits for their employees. Companies can enroll for monthly, quarterly, half-yearly or annual programs for their employees.

MiamiYoga has relied so far on word of mouth and personal referrals for expanding its business. However, the company now wants to establish a digital presence in order to reach to potential corporate customers as well. The business also wants to use a CRM system to track the interactions between its sales associates and new prospects. MiamiYoga wants to use the CRM system to close new deals faster and also to reach more prospects. The business has decided to go for HubSpot CRM because this product is available for free.

Business owners for MiamiYoga will assess the benefits derived from using HubSpot CRM before they decide on whether to purchase premium products such as Sales Hub, Marketing Hub or Service Hub.

Creating a website:

The first step towards establishing a digital presence for any business or company is to create a dedicated website. We will use the free online tool called Wix.com to create a new website for MiamiYoga. We can either create our website from scratch or we can use any of the templates that are already available on Wix.com

We will initially create a new email ID for our business. We can then use this email ID to sign up for Wix.com and also for HubSpot CRM. We will go to the new account creation page on Google and we will create a new account called as miamiyoga.hubspotdemo@gmail.com. This email ID will be the primary email ID associated with MiamiYoga. The following image displays the Gmail inbox for this email ID.

We will now go to Wix.com to register on the site with our newly created Gmail ID. The following screenshot shows the new account creation page on Wix.com.

Once we register for a new account on Wix.com, we can then create a new website for MiamiYoga on this platform. We will use a predefined template from the Health & Wellness category to create the new website.

The following screenshot displays the website template selection page on Wix.com.

We will now select the predefined template titled "Yoga Retreat" for creating our website. We can click on the Edit button by hovering over the template in order to edit the pages as required for MiamiYoga. Following image displays the same.

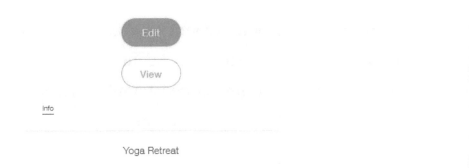

Once we click on the Edit button, a new page for Wix website editor is opened. We can edit the various pages for the website template as per the requirement for MiamiYoga. Following image shows the Wix website editor.

We will now edit the various pages for the website template as required for MiamiYoga. We will edit the main heading along with title and other elements in order to reflect the branding and messaging for MiamiYoga. Once we have edited the various layouts and texts on the template, we can preview as to how the website finally appears after editing. Subsequently, we can publish the website.

Following screenshots displays the some of the pages in the website for MiamiYoga that is published after editing the various content.

The above image displays the home page for our business. Similarly, the following page provides details about the various types of wellness programs that are offered by MiamiYoga.

We will be using the above website in subsequent topics when we will look at some of the features that are available in HubSpot CRM.

Signing up for HubSpot CRM:

We can sign up for free HubSpot CRM by initially clicking on the "Get HubSpot free" button on the HubSpot website.

We can then click on the "Get free CRM" button in the subsequent page.

We can complete the registration by providing the details such as First Name, Last Name and Email in the subsequent page. We will use the Email ID that we created earlier to access HubSpot CRM.

We need to confirm the email address that we used earlier to register with HubSpot. Once we confirm our email address, we can enter other details for HubSpot CRM such as our password, website URL and company name. Following screenshots display the relevant pages.

Step 3 of 5

Please create your password.

Password *

●●●●●●●●●●●●●●●●●●●●●● 👁

- ✓ At least 8 characters long
- ✓ One lowercase character
- ✓ One uppercase character
- ✓ One number, symbol, or whitespace character

Next

Let's get your new account set up

Website URL *

Please enter a valid website URL (ending in .com, .net, .co, .biz, .pizza, etc.)

This is between us. We won't use it to reach out to anyone else in your company.

Company name *

MiamiYoga ✓

Next

We can also provide other details about our company such as number of employees, our role in company, our designation and our awareness levels about using any type of CRM software. We will be redirected to the HubSpot CRM dashboard once we complete the registration process.

CONTACTS

Once we log in to HubSpot CRM, we can view the home page. This home page comprises of demo video that provides an overview about HubSpot CRM. The home page also comprises of a checklist of tasks that indicates the various activities that we need to complete in order to use the key features of CRM. Some of these activities are connecting the inbox, installing the sales extension, importing the data and so on. However, we can also click on the "I'll do this later" option against each of these activities if we wish to explore the various features of HubSpot CRM later at our own pace. Hence, this activity setup page is visible for new users. Users can also click on the option to skip setup that is present at the bottom of the page in order to go to the dashboard.

Following image displays the setup page displayed for new users.

The following screenshot displays the bottom section of the setup page where we have the option to skip setup for new users and to directly go to dashboard.

Frequently Asked Questions   Watch the overview video

Click here to skip setup and go to your dashboard.

The dashboard page comprises of standard reports that provide information related to marketing, sales or the service aspects of the business.

For example, following are some of the reports that are displayed within the Sales Dashboard.

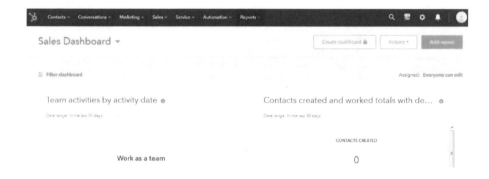

Following are some of the additional reports that are displayed within the Sales Dashboard page.

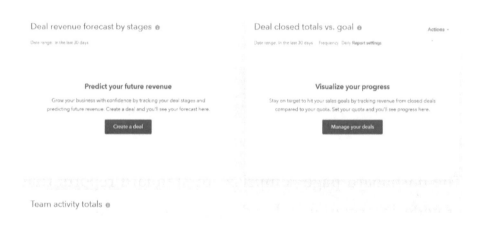

Similarly, we can view the marketing or service dashboard by clicking on the down arrow icon at the top.

For example, we can select Marketing Dashboard by clicking on the respective option as shown in the following image.

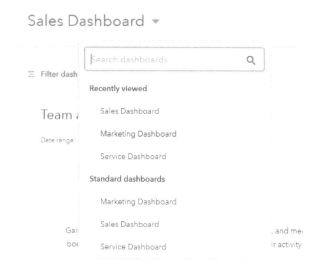

We can add more reports to Sales, Marketing or Service Dashboards by clicking on the Add report button that is located at the top of the dashboard.

Adding new contacts:

The most important asset for any business or an organization is contact. When a company interacts with an individual, that person is defined as a contact. Interaction can be of many varieties. For example, a company sales associate might have met a prospect at a trade show. This individual is defined as an unqualified lead initially. When the sales team interacts with this individual further, they can qualify this lead depending upon the chances of the company getting new business from him.

HubSpot CRM comprises of a horizontal bar at the top. This horizontal bar contains links to various pages where we can enter the relevant data for a customer.

We can view the Contacts page by clicking on the drop down menu for Contacts from the horizontal bar and then clicking on Contacts option.

Following screenshot displays a portion of the Contacts page.

As we can see, two contacts are already created by default. We can add a new contact by clicking on the "Create Contact" button.

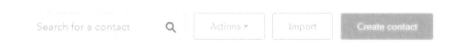

We will now add the contact details of an individual customer who has enrolled for annual wellness program with MiamiYoga. We can enter various details for the new contact such as Email, First name, Last name, Contact owner, phone number and so on from the Create Contact page. We can also assign Lifecycle stage for any contact while entering the details. Lifecycle stage indicates as to whether a contact is a lead, sales qualified lead, opportunity or a customer and so on. In this case, we will select the Lifecycle stage for our new contact as Customer. Similarly, we can also assign a value for Lead status to indicate as to whether a lead is new, unqualified or connected and so on. Lifecycle stage and Lead status enables us to understand the level of interaction that a business currently has with a contact.

Following screenshots displays the Create contact page that contains the details of the customer for MiamiYoga.

We can click on "Create contact" button to store the details of the new contact. We can also click on "Create and add another" button if we want to immediately store the details of another contact after creating the first contact.

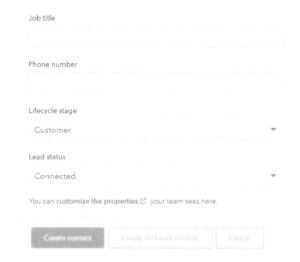

We can now view the details of the new contact as shown in the following screenshot.

We can view the details of any contact by clicking on the contact name.

Following image shows the detail page for the contact that we created in the previous steps.

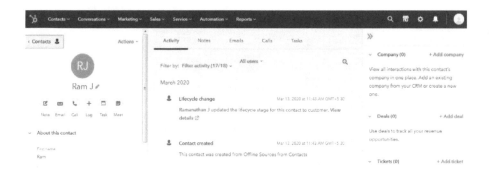

A key aspect of customer relationship management is to keep track of all the interactions that company employees have with a contact. The contact detail page is the single source of reference for maintaining a record of all interactions between company employees and the contact.

We can edit the data or include additional information for a contact from the contact details page itself. We can click on a field and then enter the necessary details. We can then click on Save button to update the contact details. For example, let us enter the phone number for our newly created contact from the contact details page.

As soon as we edit the phone number field for our contact, we can see a horizontal prompt with Save and Cancel buttons.

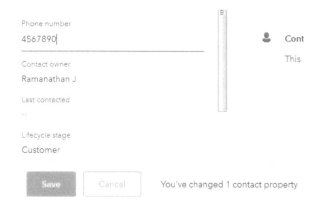

We can click on Save to update the contact details. To delete a contact, we can click on the Delete button within the Actions menu.

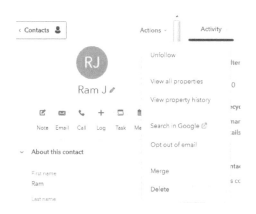

Creating activity related record for a contact:

We can make the contact detail record more valuable by storing additional information that is related to the individual. For example, we can log call activity for a contact or emails that we may have sent to this contact from the details page. We can create notes for a contact in order to keep track of important information. We can also create a task for ourselves or our teammates. This set of tasks can serve as a to-do list for a contact.

Logging Email:

We can log emails that we have sent to a contact by clicking on the Log Email button within the Emails section of the contact detail page. When we log the email activity for a contact, we can provide details such as to whom we sent the email, when we sent the email and a description of the email content.

For example, let us create a log for email that we have sent before to our newly created contact Ran J. This email was about a new referral scheme for MiamiYoga customers.

Following screenshot displays the Emails section within the Contact details page.

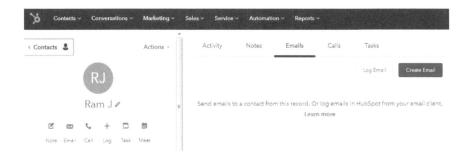

We can describe email activity in a new window when we click on the Log Email button in the Emails section for the Contact Details page.

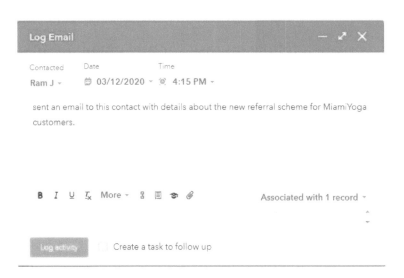

We can click on Log activity button to store the email activity for the contact. Subsequently, we can view the log detail in the Emails section for a contact.

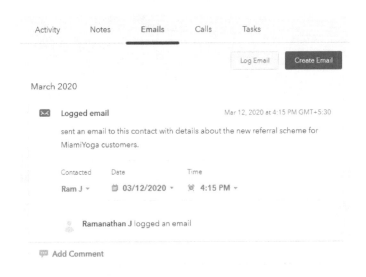

We can also create a follow up task for any email log that we create for a contact by clicking on the "Create a task to follow up" check box next to the Log activity button. We can also assign a due date for this task.

Subsequently, when we go to the Tasks section within the Contact details page, we can view the follow up task that we created while storing the email log for the contact.

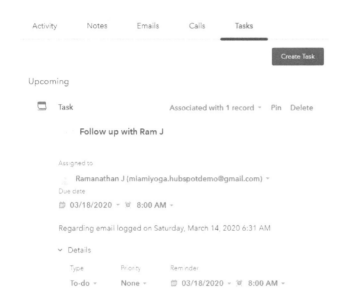

We can assign additional details for the follow up task such as Type, Priority or Reminder. The task type can be Call, Email or To-do. Similarly, we can assign a High priority value to a task if required. We can also assign a date and time for reminder if required. All activities such as creating email log or follow up tasks appear in the Activity section for a Contact.

Create Email:

We can send emails from CRM itself by connecting our email account to HubSpot. We can connect Gmail, Office 365 or other IMAP based email accounts with HubSpot.

For our case study, we are using a Gmail based email account for our MiamiYoga business. We will connect this email account with HubSpot CRM. We can click on the "Create Email" button that is located within the Emails section of the Contact details page.

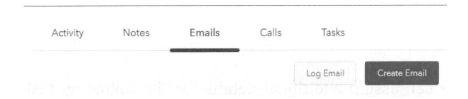

We can then select any of the email accounts to connect with HubSpot CRM in the subsequent page. Since we are using Gmail based account for MiamiYoga, we will select Connect Gmail option to connect our email account with HubSpot.

Once we connect our Gmail account to HubSpot, other Google services such as Google Calendar, Google Drive, and Google Search Console will be linked to HubSpot as well. We can now click on Connect Gmail link as shown in the above screenshot. We will then be asked to enter our Gmail credentials in the subsequent page.

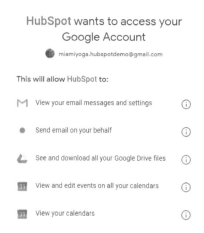

We can click on Allow to enable HubSpot integration with our Gmail account. Once we have linked HubSpot CRM with our Gmail account, we will be redirected to HubSpot from where we can now directly send emails to our contacts.

The following screenshot displays the Create Email page that can be accessed from Emails section in Contact Details page within HubSpot CRM.

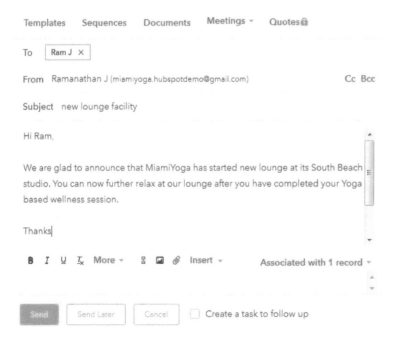

We can either send the email immediately or we can schedule to send the email later by clicking on Send Later button. Once we click on Send, the email will also be available as a record within the Activity and Emails section of the Contact Details page.

The following screenshot shows the Activity section of the Contact Details page.

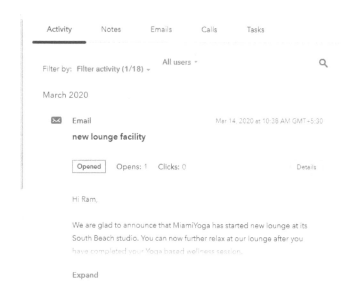

Similarly, following screenshot shows the Emails section within the Contact Details page.

Once we send an email from HubSpot CRM, this email will also be visible in the Sent email of our Gmail account.

HubSpot CRM provides Email tracking feature that can let us know as to when the recipient or contact has opened the email that we have sent. We can view the Email tracking details from the Activity section of the Contact details page. For example, let us assume that our newly created contact Ram J has opened the email regarding the new lounge facility at MiamiYoga. If we now go to the Activity section in contact details page, we can view the Email tracking details.

Following screenshot displays the email tracking related messages within the Activity section.

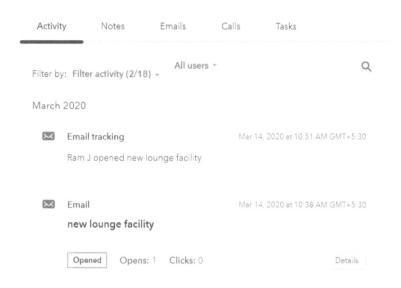

The email tracking message states that the contact has opened the email with the respective subject line. Similarly, the Email activity log displays the status as "Opened". The "Opens" value is shown as one. This indicates the number of times the contact opened the email. Similarly, if we have included any hyperlinks or URLs in our email, we can track the number of times the contact has clicked on them from the "Clicks" value.

Adding Notes to Contacts:

We can add notes for any contact in order to store any additional information. We can create a new note for a contact by clicking on the Create Note button within the Notes section in the contact detail page. We can even mention our team members in the note by including @ symbol in front of the team member name.

Following screenshot displays the Notes section within the contact detail page.

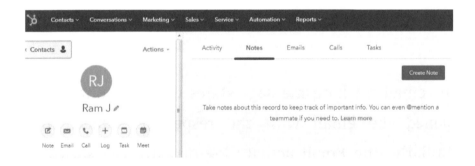

We can enter the description for the note in the subsequent page after we click on the Create Note button. As we saw in case of Emails, we can also create follow up tasks when we create notes for any contact.

Following image displays the page to enter note description for any contact.

We can click on Save note to create the new note. We can now view this note in the Activity and the Notes section within the contact detail page. We can edit the note that we have already created by clicking on the note description within the Activity or the Notes section and then entering any new details for the note. We can then click on the Save button to update the note.

Log Calls:

We can log a call activity for a contact to keep track of our discussion. We can click on the Log Call button within the Calls section of the contact detail page to store the call activity for a contact.

Following image displays the log call page.

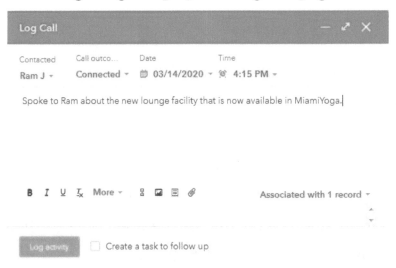

We can also store the outcomes for various call attempts by selecting the suitable option from the Call outcome menu in the Log Call page. Some of the options for Call outcome include Connected, Busy and Left voicemail. We can store the record by clicking on Log activity.

As we saw in case of Email and Notes, we can also create a follow up task for call activity if required. The log call activity is now visible in the Calls and Activity section of the contact details page.

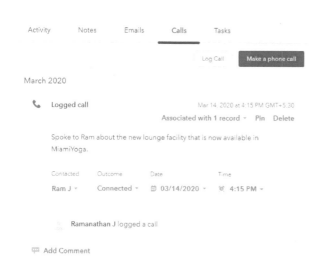

Make a phone call:

We can directly call contacts from phone or web browser when we register our phone number with HubSpot CRM. Calls are directly recorded to the CRM thereby ensuring that all our conversations are stored in one place.

We can click on "Make a phone call" button within the Calls section. Subsequently, we need to click on Add your phone number button as shown in the following image.

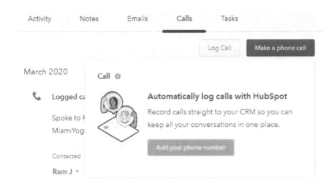

We can then enter our phone number to receive a call with registration code.

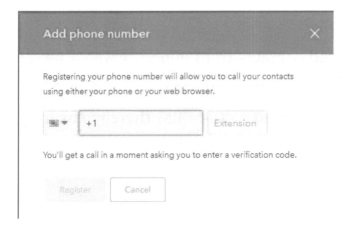

Import Contacts:

We may often store contact data in various forms across several devices. For e.g. we can export contact data from our Android phones to our computers in the form of CSV or Excel files. Similarly, we can export contact data from our email account to our computer in Excel file format. Many of the contact data records could be related to our business and hence we would want to upload this data to HubSpot CRM in order to keep track of all the relevant contacts.

We can import contact data to HubSpot CRM by clicking on the Import button that is located in the Contacts page.

We can format our contact data file by including standard columns such as First Name, Last Name, Email, Phone Number and Lead Status before we begin the import process.

Once we click on the Import button as shown in the previous image, we will be led to another page from where we can start the data import process. This page also gives more information about how to prepare our spreadsheet for data import process.

The data import wizard will display the next steps in corresponding pages when we click on the Start an import button as shown in the previous image. We have created a sample contact data file that is in the form of an Excel file. We will be importing this contact data file to HubSpot. The data import process remains the same when we upload contact, company, deal, ticket or product data. We will select the File from computer option from the subsequent page and then click on Next. The following image displays the same.

What would you like to import?

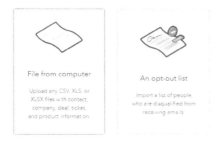

File from computer

Upload any CSV, XLS, or
XLSX files with contact,
company, deal, ticket,
and product information.

An opt-out list

Import a list of people
who are disqualified from
receiving emails.

Need help getting started? **View import guide** 🗗

We can select in the next step as to how many files we are uploading for data import. We will choose the One file option for our current example and then click on Next.

TYPE   UPLOAD   MAP   DETAILS

How many files are you importing?

You can upload one file or multiple files at a time. You'll be able to choose
how many objects you're importing later.

One file

Multiple files with
associations

HubSpot CRM organizes information into various objects. Some of the common objects include contacts, companies and deals. We mention in the next step of the data import process as to how many types of object data that are we uploading. For our example, we are importing only contact object data and hence we choose the One object option.

In the subsequent step, we will specify Contacts as the specific object for which we are importing the data. In case if we are importing data for other objects, we can select the other option such as Companies, Deals or Tickets.

We can upload the contact file data in the next step.

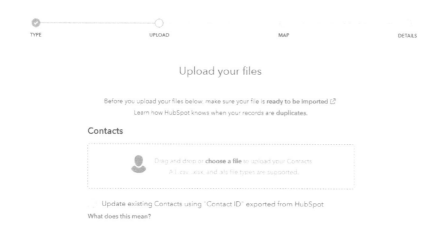

HubSpot CRM maintains information about any object in the form of Properties. When we import any object data, we can map the columns from our file to object properties. In case there is any unmatched column in our file, we can choose to not to select that column for import.

The following screenshot displays the column mapping page from the data import wizard process.

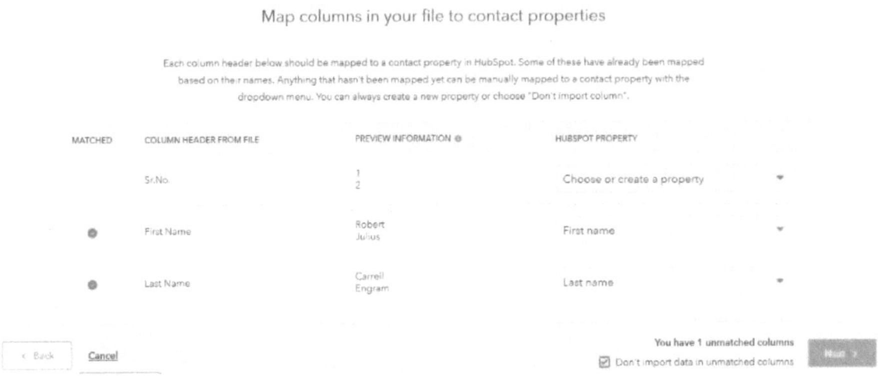

Map columns in your file to contact properties

Each column header below should be mapped to a contact property in HubSpot. Some of these have already been mapped based on their names. Anything that hasn't been mapped yet can be manually mapped to a contact property with the dropdown menu. You can always create a new property or choose "Don't import column".

MATCHED	COLUMN HEADER FROM FILE	PREVIEW INFORMATION	HUBSPOT PROPERTY
	Sr.No.	1 2	Choose or create a property
●	First Name	Robert Julius	First name
●	Last Name	Carrell Engram	Last name

‹ Back   Cancel

You have 1 unmatched columns
☑ Don't import data in unmatched columns   Next ›

We can also manually assign any unmatched column to a HubSpot property if required. The Sr.No. or Serial Number from our contact data file is the unmatched column in our example. We will choose to not to import the serial number data from the contact file.

We can assign a name to the data import process in the subsequent process. We select the options to create a list of contacts from the import. We also select the option for declaring that we have a prior relationship with the contacts and that the contact data was not purchased, rented or provided by a third party.

We click on the Finish Import button to complete the data import process.

Once we have imported the data, we can view the log for the contact data import process. We can view details such as number of new records, updated records and any errors for the data import from the log.

NAME	NEW RECORDS ⊖	UPDATED RECORDS ⊖	ERROR COUNT ⊖	SOURCE	USER	CREATED
Contact Contacts	2		0	File	Ramanathan J	03/14/2020 9:35 PM
ContactData Contacts	2		0	File	Ramanathan J	03/14/2020 8:31 PM

We can now view the imported data in the Contacts page.

The object data file that is to be imported has to be formatted according to the relevant properties for the object in HubSpot CRM. However, the data import process remains the same for all objects in HubSpot CRM.

Create custom property:

HubSpot CRM offers certain standard properties to store information about any object. For e.g. First Name, Last Name, Email, Phone Number are some of the standard properties that are available in HubSpot CRM to store information for contact object. However, on many instances we may have additional information that we want to store for an object. In these cases, the standard properties for an object may not be sufficient. We can create new properties to store other information for an object in HubSpot CRM.

For example, MiamiYoga offers Yoga based wellness programs to customers. These wellness programs were earlier available to only individual customers. Now, MiamiYoga plans to offer wellness solutions to companies as well. As a result, companies can send their employees to MiamiYoga studio on a weekly basis in order to participate in various wellness programs.

The owners of MiamiYoga now want to differentiate a lead as to whether the person is likely to do business with MiamiYoga as an individual or whether he/she will represent a company to whom corporate wellness programs can be offered. Similarly, the business owners would like to know as to whether a current customer has subscribed to wellness programs as an individual or whether he/she represents a company which in turn has subscribed to wellness programs for its employees.

The standard properties that are available for Contact object in HubSpot CRM may not be sufficient to distinguish the type of contact. Hence, we will create a new property named "Account Type" that will indicate as to whether a contact represents individual or a company. As a result, Account Type custom property will have two values i.e. Individual or Corporate.

We can create new property for the Contact object by clicking on Edit properties option from the Actions menu in the Contacts page.

We will then be redirected to the Settings page where we can view all properties that are available for various objects. We can set filter values to view the specific properties as per our requirements. For example, we can filter by properties for various objects, groups, field types or users. Properties are stored in various groups such as Company properties, Contact properties, Deal properties and Ticket properties.

We will now click on the Create property button in the Settings page.

We can provide basic information about a property in the subsequent page.

We can provide field type and label values in the subsequent page. We choose "Dropdown select" as the field type and label values as "Individual" and "Corporate" for the Account Type custom property.

We can see the preview of the custom property in the Create a new property page itself. We can also choose as to whether we want the custom property to be displayed in forms.

We can click on Create to store the new property. We can now view the custom property in the list of properties from the Settings page.

If we now go to the Contact details page, we can observe that our new custom property is not visible for any contact. We can enable the new custom property for a contact by clicking on View all properties from the left pane in the Contact details page.

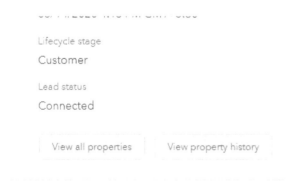

Subsequently, we can click on the Add to your view button for our custom property.

We can observe that the new custom property is now visible for the Contact object.

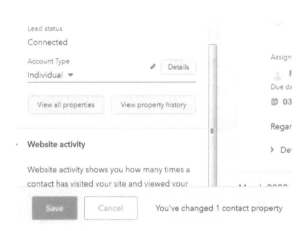

Create a company:

We observed earlier that many contacts are often associated with companies. Some of the leads could represent organizations from whom we are trying to get business. Similarly, other contacts could represent companies who would be already doing business with us.

When we create a new contact in HubSpot CRM, a corresponding company record for the contact is automatically created. We can also create a new company record from the Companies page. We can access the Companies page from the Contacts menu as shown in the following image.

The following screenshot displays the Companies page.

We can observe that some of the company records were already created when we stored the records for new contacts earlier. We can click on Create company button to store new company record.

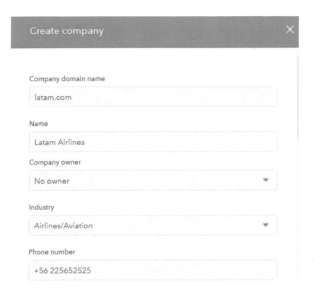

When we enter the company domain name in the Create company page, other details such as Company name, industry, phone number, city, state, description and LinkedIn company page are automatically filled. We can edit or enter other details such as Type and then click on Create company button to store the new company record.

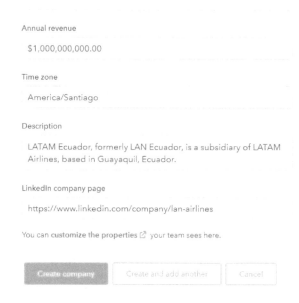

We can view the newly created company record in the Companies page. We can click on any company record to view the company details page.

Following screenshot displays the Companies page.

Following image displays the Company details page.

We can observe that Company details page also have Activity, Notes, Emails, Calls and Tasks sections similar to those in the Contact details page.

CONVERSATIONS

Any business will interact with customers or prospects on numerous occasions through various means. Some of these interactions could happen over the phone whereas other conversations can take place through digital platforms such as Emails or Chat applications.

HubSpot CRM offers the Inbox feature which we can use to manage all our conversations in one place. We can connect our email, forms, chat and Facebook messenger with HubSpot Inbox in order to obtain a holistic view of all the interactions that are happening between our business and the various contacts. Businesses can now connect to HubSpot CRM Inbox in order to get an overview of various conversations and to prioritize the response for various contacts.

Connecting Email Channel:

We can open the HubSpot Inbox from the Conversations menu that is located at the top horizontal bar.

We can click on the Email option to connect this channel with HubSpot Inbox.

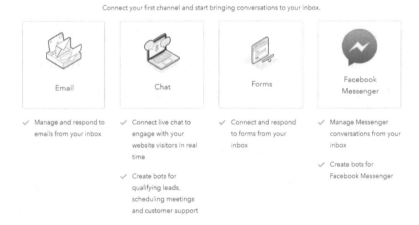

We will now connect our MiamiYoga email account with HubSpot Inbox. We connect our email to conversations inbox as a shared account. Everyone who has access to conversations inbox can view shared accounts.

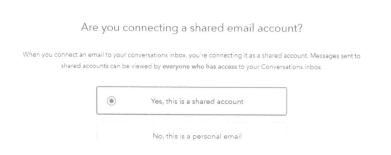

We will select the Gmail as the team email option in the subsequent page.

We will select the MiamiYoga Gmail ID in the subsequent page. We can then allow HubSpot access to the MiamiYoga email account. Subsequently, we can customize our email details such as whether we want to display only company name in From or whether we want to display both agent and company name. We can also enable team signature if required.

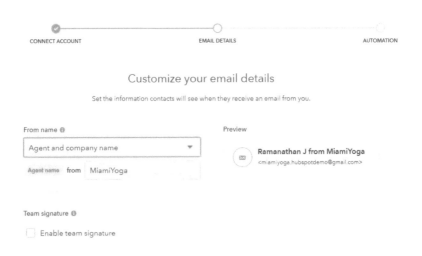

We can also automatically create a ticket every time a new email is sent to our account if required. We can click on Connect & finish button to complete the linking of our email account with HubSpot CRM.

We can view the Inbox that is now connected to our MiamiYoga Gmail account.

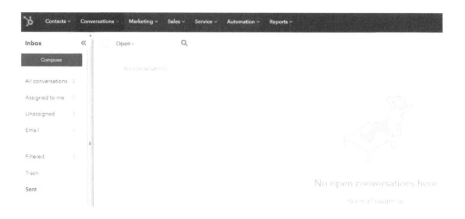

Create snippets:

We can improve the speed with which we write emails and take notes by creating shortcuts to our most common responses for emails that we sent to prospects as well as for notes that we log in the CRM. We can create snippets that we can use to quickly send emails and to log notes by avoiding the need to type the same content again.

We can access the page to create new snippets by clicking on the Snippets option from the Conversations menu.

We can click on Create snippet button in the subsequent page to store the new snippet in the CRM.

We can enter details such as Internal name, Snippet text and Shortcut in the New snippet page. In this case, we are creating a new snippet that introduces MiamiYoga. We can use this snippet whenever we want to compose emails before sending them to prospects. We can create a snippet shortcut by entering a text after the default # symbol in the page for creating new snippet. We can use this snippet shortcut by typing # symbol followed by the snippet shortcut text.

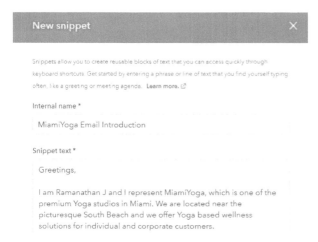

The following screenshot displays the portion of New snippet page where we can enter the text for snippet shortcut.

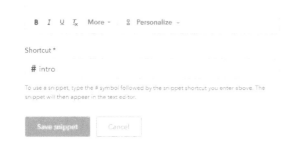

We can store the new snippet data by clicking on Save snippet button as shown in the previous screenshot. We can view the list of snippets that we have created from the Snippets home page.

We can create folders to organize our snippets according to content or purpose. We can modify any snippet by clicking on the snippet name to open the Edit snippet page.

Using Snippets:

We can use snippets in our email by entering the # symbol followed by the snippet shortcut text that we entered when we created the snippet in the previous step.

For example, suppose we want to send an email that describes about the wellness programs offered by MiamiYoga to one of our leads. We can click on the lead name from the Contacts page in order to open the Contact details page. Subsequently, we can click on Create Email button from the Emails section to compose a new email.

We can insert the snippet for the introduction text that we created earlier in this email by typing # symbol followed by snippet shortcut text. In this case, our snippet shortcut is #intro. We can select the snippet from the prompt when we enter the shortcut.

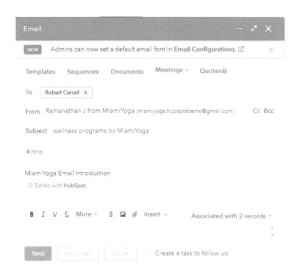

When we select the snippet, the corresponding text is automatically inserted in the email. Following screenshot displays the compose email window after selecting the snippet text.

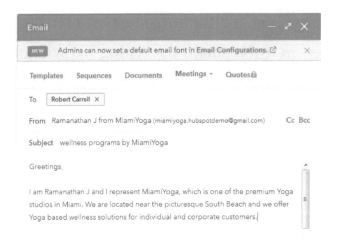

We can quickly compose emails by using different types of snippet shortcuts.

Create Templates:

We can save repetitive email content as an email template. We can select an email template and then customize the content according to the recipients. We can access these templates from HubSpot CRM or when we send an email from the Inbox.

Users of free HubSpot CRM can access up to first five templates.

We can access Templates page from the Conversations menu.

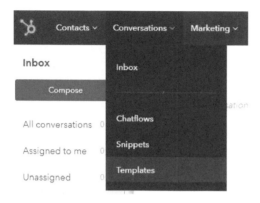

We can click on the New Template button from Templates page to create a new template. We can either create a new template from scratch or we can use any of the templates that are already available in the template library.

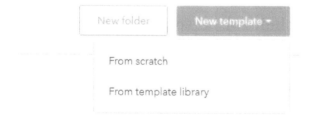

We can click on From scratch option to create a new template.

The following screenshot displays the new template creation page.

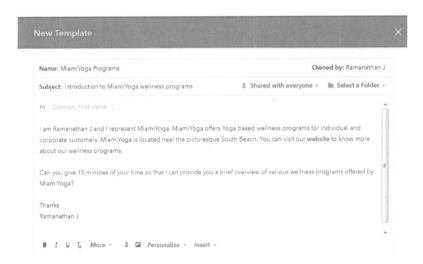

We can customize email templates by inserting personalization tokens. We can click on Personalize menu from the New template page to insert these tokens. For example, we have included a personalization token for contact first name at the top when we created our new template. As a result, the first name that is to be included in the email template will be customized according to the corresponding value for the Contact. We can similarly insert personalization token for other objects such as Company, Sender or Deal.

Similarly, we can insert URL or images in our template as per our requirement. We can also include Snippets, Documents or Meeting Links in our email template if we would like to.

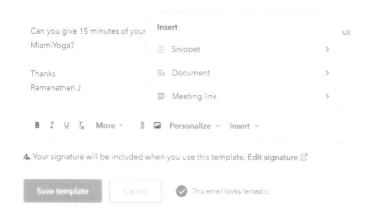

We can click on Save template button to store our template. We can view our newly created template in the Templates page. We can also create a new folder to organize our templates as required.

We can click on any existing template to update its contents.

Create Chatflows:

We can create custom chat experiences for visitors who are browsing our company website or Facebook pages with the Chatflows functionality. We can use Chatflows to build welcome message that can greet visitors or to direct them to live team. We can also use Chatflows to build bots for qualifying leads or to design virtual assistants that can support customers.

We can access Chatflows page from the Conversations menu.

We can click on Create chatflow button from the Chatflows page to store the new chatflow for our website or for our Facebook page.

We can select in the next step as to where we would like to add this chatflow. We can deploy the chatflow to our website or to the Facebook page. When we connect a Facebook page to HubSpot CRM, we can add chatflow to Facebook Messenger. For our case study, we will choose to add chatflow to our MiamiYoga website.

We will initially need to add live chat to our website. This live chat can have various purposes such as to welcome visitors and then send them directly to our business team or to qualify visitors as potential leads before redirecting them to our sales associates and so on. We will choose to create a new live chat that will welcome visitors.

Create chatflow

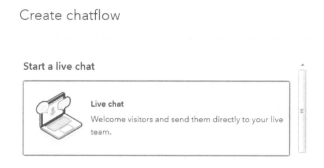

We can edit the welcome message as required in the subsequent step named Build.

We can also specify in this step whether we want to ask visitors for their email address. For example, if no team member responds to visitor's message after one minute, we can ask visitors to leave their email address.

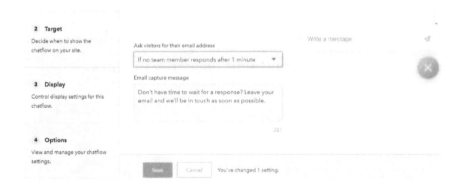

We can click on Save to store our settings.

The next step for creating a chatflow is called Target. We can assign rules to decide for which web pages the chatflow will be displayed. We can also determine when to display the chatflow depending upon visitor identity or behavior. In this case, we would want the chatflow to be visible for all pages in our website.

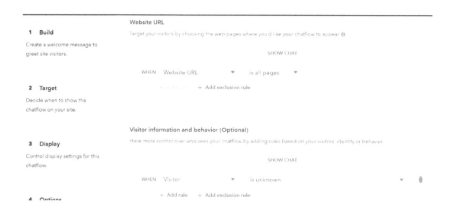

We can click on Save to store the settings for this step.

The next step for creating a chatflow is called Display. We can customize the chat heading, chat display behavior and timing controls in this step. We will assign the name MiamiYoga Bot for our new chatflow. We will also use our logo as a custom picture for the chat application.

We can also determine in this step as to how the chat widget will look like when the visitors access our website. For example, we can open the welcome message as a prompt, we can show the chat launcher or we can open the chat message window itself. Similarly, we can also decide as to when the chat welcome message should be displayed to the visitors.

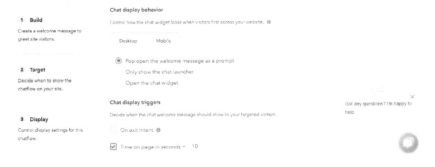

We can save the settings and proceed to the next step named Display. In this step, we can select a language for the chatflow. We can also include in this step data privacy and consent messages that are to be displayed to visitors if required.

We can now view the chatflow that we have just created in the Chatflows page.

We can click on the Switch button in the Status column to change its Status value for the chatflow.

Installing tracking code:

We need to install the tracking code on our website in order to let HubSpot know where the chatflow should appear. We can click on Get tracking code button at the top of the Chatflows page to open the Tracking code page for chat.

We can copy the tracking code for chat and paste it into every page of our website where we want the chat to appear. We need to place the code just before the end of <body> tag for our web page.

The following screenshot displays the tracking code page for chat.

We can also email the code snippet to other individual such as web developer or administrator in order to allow them to install the code.

Deploying Chatflows:

As we observed earlier, we get a tracking code when we create a chatflow in HubSpot CRM. We need to insert this tracking code in every page of our website where we want the chat application to appear. We can open the HTML page of our website through the corresponding editor. For our case study, we used the popular online website builder tool wix.com to create a new website for MiamiYoga. The online tool wix.com also has a tool for adding tracking code to pages from our website. This tool is available for users who have purchased the premium plan for their websites on wix.com.

Following screenshot displays the Settings page within wix.com for adding tracking code to our website.

We can upgrade our plan on wix.com in order to place the tracking code for each page in our website. Subsequently, we can click on the Custom tracking tool option as shown in the following image in order to add the chatflow tracking code to required pages of our MiamiYoga website.

We can place the tracking code for our chatflow in the subsequent page for pasting code in wix.com. We can add the code to all pages of our website or we can select specific pages where we want our chatflow to appear. We will choose Home, About and Programs pages from the MiamiYoga website for displaying the chat application. Similarly, we can also choose where we want to place code.

The following screenshot displays the page from the online editor wix.com where we can insert the tracking code for our chat application. We can click on Apply to deploy the chat tracking code in specific pages of our website.

The tracking tool and analytics page from Wix.com will now show the portion where we have deployed the chat tracking code.

Following screenshot displays the MiamiYoga website where the new chatflow is now deployed.

Chatflows can be one of the most effective ways to communicate with visitors. HubSpot CRM users who subscribe for upgraded product features such as Service Hub Professional can create support bot chatflow that can display knowledge articles to customers or can empower these visitors to create a ticket for resolving support issues.

SALES HUB – DEALS

Any prospect or lead goes through certain stages or steps before he/she decides to purchase a product or service from a business. Business owners can track their prospects across various stages of this decision making process.

Customer buying process is represented as Deals in HubSpot CRM. Business owners can track their sales with Deals. Sales process is classified into multiple stages in HubSpot. We can drag and drop the various deals into these stages as our sales process moves forward with individual prospects. Deals in HubSpot CRM comprises of some default stages. However, we can customize the deal stages according to the sales process that is followed by our business.

Modifying Deal Stages:

We can access the Deals page from the Sales menu in HubSpot CRM.

The Deals page comprises of certain default deal stages such as Appointment scheduled, Qualified to buy, Presentation scheduled, Decision maker bought-in and so on. We can modify these deal stages to reflect the customer buying process in our organization.

These deal stages can reflect the necessary steps that customer will take to evaluate the product or service before he/she does business with an organization.

For example, let us consider the possible steps or stages an individual prospect or lead for our MiamiYoga business would consider before he/she subscribes to one of the wellness programs that are offered by our business.

The prospect or lead can come to know about MiamiYoga through many possible ways. For instance, the prospect can visit the MiamiYoga website after searching on Google for Yoga studios in Miami. The prospect could have seen a post, comment or an ad that would have mentioned MiamiYoga on any of the social media platforms. Finally, the prospect could have heard about MiamiYoga through referral by one of the existing customers.

Once the prospect visits the MiamiYoga website, he/she will read the information about various aspects such as the location of Yoga studio, profile of Yoga instructors and description of various wellness programs that are offered by the business. The prospect can then approach MiamiYoga through phone, email or chat to obtain more information about the various facilities and wellness programs that are offered by the business. The prospect is now actively evaluating the services that are offered by MiamiYoga. We can term this deal stage as Active program evaluation. This deal stage helps us to differentiate between the passive visitors who just browse through the content that is available on MiamiYoga website and active prospects who consider the website as an initial step to know more about MiamiYoga before they approach the business over the phone or email to obtain more information about the various wellness programs and the facilities that are available.

Once the business associates at MiamiYoga receive a call or email from the prospect seeking more information about any aspect of the business, these associates can then provide the corresponding details to the prospect.

Subsequently, the business associates can also ask the prospect as to whether he/she would like to visit the MiamiYoga studio at a convenient schedule in order to personally look at the various facilities that are available at the Yoga studio. The business associates can seek to book a meeting slot for the prospect. Thus, we can term this deal stage as Provide details and offer studio visit.

The prospect can then visit the MiamiYoga studio to observe the various aspects of the wellness programs and the location. This is a distinct stage in the customer buying process and can be termed as Prospect visits studio. The prospect can now ask further queries about the various wellness programs and pricing at this stage.

The prospect would possibly take some time now to decide upon whether to purchase any of the wellness programs. Some prospects may decide to purchase a wellness program when they visit the MiamiYoga studio. We can identify two stages namely Closed won and Closed lost at this point. These two stages mark the completion of customer buying process. These two stages indicate whether the company got the business from a prospect or whether the company was unable to close the deal.

We can edit the deal stages in HubSpot CRM to reflect the customer buying process for MiamiYoga. Following are the deal stages for MiamiYoga business that we will create in HubSpot CRM.

1. Active program evaluation
2. Provide details and offer studio visit
3. Prospect visits studio
4. Closed won
5. Closed lost

We can click on Edit deal stages link from the Actions menu in the Deals page to modify the deal stages as per the customer buying process for our organization.

We can edit the deal stages that are presently described in the Deals settings page. We can also assign a win probability percentage to each deal stage. We can assign this percentage value based upon our understanding of the likelihood that a prospect will enter into a deal with our business when he/she reaches a certain stage in the buying process.

We can assign the deal stages and the corresponding win probability percentage values in the Deals settings page as shown in the following screenshot.

We can edit properties for each deal stage if required. We can click on Save to store the deal stages.

We can now view the updated deal stages from the Deals page in Sales Hub.

As we can see in the above screenshot, the new deal stages in HubSpot CRM now reflect the customer buying process for MiamiYoga.

The free version of HubSpot CRM provides one sales pipeline for which we can create or edit deal stages. If we want to create multiple sales pipelines, we need to subscribe to Sales Hub Starter version.

For example, we observed earlier that MiamiYoga plans to sell its wellness programs to corporate customers as well. In case of corporate customers, there will be additional deal stages for the customer buying process.

Corporate customers will need to seek budget approval from the key decision makers in their organization before they can subscribe for wellness programs from MiamiYoga for the employees.

Create Deals:

We can store new deals in HubSpot CRM by clicking on the Create deal button in the Deals page.

We can track various business deals that are in progress with different prospects by creating respective deals for them. Each of these deals can be at different deal stages. For e.g. one deal could be at the Active program evaluation deal stage while other deal could be at the Prospect visits studio deal stage. Similarly, we can assign the amount value to these deals. This amount can represent the potential business value of a particular deal. We can also assign close date, deal owner and deal type values to the new deal that we create in HubSpot CRM.

Deal type indicates as to whether the current deal represents new business or whether the deal is for existing business. Finally, we can allocate the deal with a company or a contact from the CRM. Users who have subscribed for Sales Hub Professional version can also add a product to a deal. Sales Hub Professional users can create a product library from where they can assign products to a deal.

For example, we will now create a new deal for one of the contact who is a prospect. We are trying to seek new business from this prospect for MiamiYoga.

This prospect has approached MiamiYoga by email and has sought more details about various wellness programs. Sales associates have provided the relevant information to this prospect and have offered him a studio visit. Hence, the current deal stage for this prospect is Provide details and offer studio visit. We can assign an approximate amount to the Amount field based upon our estimate of the potential business value.

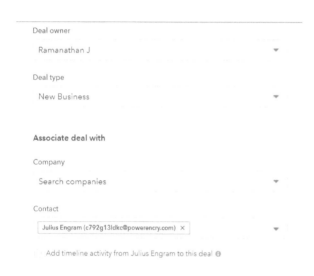

Deal owner field value represents the associate from our business who is pursuing the deal with a prospect. We can assign accountability by allocating an owner to each deal.

We can indicate whether a deal represents new business or existing business by assigning a value to the Deal type field. In this case, we assign the New business value to the Deal type field because we are trying to win business from this prospect for the first time.

We can associate the deal with a Company and/or a Contact by assigning the corresponding values. For example, if we are pursuing a deal with a corporate customer, we can assign a Company value to the deal as well as the name of the person from the company with whom we are interacting as the Contact value.

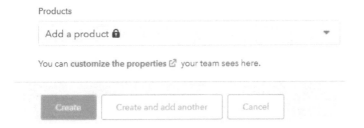

As mentioned earlier, Sales Hub Professional users can store product values in product library and can then assign these products to deals. We can click on Create to store the new deal.

We can now view the deal that we have created in the Deals page.

The deal is stored in the corresponding deal stage column. We can drag and drop this deal across deal various stages to reflect the progress in our interactions with a prospect. For example, suppose our prospect visits the MiamiYoga studio after some days to view the facilities in person. We can then update the deal stage value for this deal to "Prospect visits studio" by drag dropping the deal to the appropriate deal stage column.

We can click on any deal to view the Deal details page as shown in the following screenshot.

The Deal details page displays the activity history for any deal. We can also create notes, make a phone call or log a phone call record, create an email or log an email record and create task for a deal from the Deal details page.

In this way, we can create multiple deals in HubSpot CRM to keep a track of business opportunities that we pursue with multiple prospects at any instant. The column total value for each deal stage indicates the total amount of potential sales revenue that is currently present in any deal stage. Hence, business owners can also refer to the Deals dashboard in order to identify bottlenecks that might be affecting the sales process in an organization.

The following screenshot shows the Deals page with multiple deals. The Prospect visits studio deal stage column comprise of two deals with a total potential sales revenue of USD 8000.

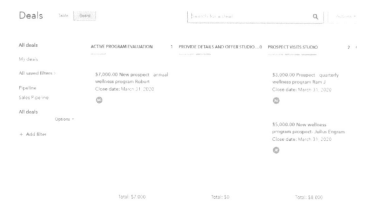

The Deals page can be displayed in the Board or Table format. Board format enables users to drag and drop deals across various stages in the Deals page. Following screenshot displays the Deals page in the Table format.

SALES HUB – TASKS

We have observed earlier that we can create tasks for contacts, companies or deals through the details page for these objects in HubSpot CRM. Similarly, we can also create tasks that can serve as reminders for our team from the Tasks page in Sales Hub. Business owners can follow up with their team members to complete various activities such as to send emails or to make calls to prospects by creating dedicated tasks for the same from the Tasks page.

Tasks can be of various types such as To-dos, Emails or Calls. We can classify a task as High priority if required. We can also filter records in the Tasks page according to various criteria such as Open tasks, Due today, Due this week or Overdue.

Create task from Tasks page:

We can access the Tasks page from the Sales Hub menu as shown in the following image.

Following screenshot describes the Tasks page.

We can click on the Create task button to store a new task for our team. For example, we will create one task to search prospects from an airline company contact to whom we can present corporate wellness programs offered by MiamiYoga.

The following screenshot shows the page to create new task.

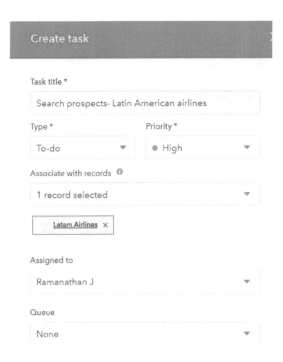

A task is usually assigned to a team member. We can associate the task with various types of records or objects such as Companies, Contacts or Deals. In this case, we have associated the task with a company contact record. We can allocate multiple types of objects to a task. For example, we can assign both company contact and a deal object to a task if required.

We can set reminders, assign due date as well as time and enter notes for the task if required. We can click on Create button to store the new task.

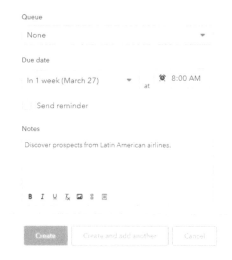

We can now see the list of open tasks in the Tasks page. We can select any task and click on the tick mark icon or the Mark as completed option to set the task status as Complete.

Create Queue:

We can create a task queue to bunch together a set of activities that we need to complete in sequence. For e.g. let us assume that we are presently seeking new business for MiamiYoga. This would require us to initially discover leads from an industry or sector. Then we need to send an initial introduction email to these prospects. Subsequently, we will then send a follow up email in a couple of days and then finally we will try to call these prospects. We can create separate tasks for each of these activities in a queue.

We can click on Add a queue link in the Queues section from the Tasks page to create a new queue.

QUEUES

Prospect Queue

+ Add a queue

Once we create a new queue, we can add tasks to this queue.

Following screenshot displays the task queue page.

We can click on Create task button to add a new task to this queue.

We can assign this new task to the corresponding queue.

We can activate a queue by clicking on Start queue from the Tasks page.

We need to assign the individual tasks in a queue to an appropriate object such as company, contact or deal before we start a task queue. In this case, we have assigned the tasks to a company record as shown in the following image.

We can now click on the Start queue button to activate the task queue. We will now be redirected to the company details page from where we can view the individual tasks for a queue.

Following screenshot displays the details page for the company to which we allocated tasks from the queue.

We can reschedule, skip or mark a task from the queue as complete for a company. We can click on the Progress menu to view other tasks from the queue.

We can assign a sequence to a set of tasks by allocating them to a task queue. We can start this queue when we assign the individual tasks to a record or an object such as company, contact or deals. We can view the individual tasks in queue from the object detail page. Once we mark a task from the queue as Complete, this task is automatically removed from the queue and is marked as Completed. We can view the completed tasks by clicking on the Completed filter from the Tasks details page.

SALES HUB- DOCUMENTS

Any business owner will deal with a lot of documents when he/she engages with various customers. These documents can include product or service brochure, presentation files, contracts and so on. HubSpot Sales Hub provides a space where users can build a library of content that is simple to share and track. Users can upload documents to HubSpot Documents space and can then share these documents through CRM or connected inbox.

We can access the Documents page from the Sales menu. We can upload documents from local drive or other cloud storage platforms such as Dropbox, Google Drive or Box to the Documents page.

Following screenshot displays the Documents page.

We can upload documents to HubSpot by clicking on the Upload new document button as shown in the above image. For example, we will upload a presentation document that describes the various wellness programs that are offered by MiamiYoga. We will upload this presentation from the local drive. The Documents page will list all the documents that are uploaded to HubSpot.

Free users for HubSpot CRM can upload five documents. Users who subscribe for Sales Hub Starter version can upload more documents.

We can click on the link for any document that we have uploaded in the Documents page to view the corresponding metrics.

We can view the total links created, number of visitors and views for a document from the document details page. We can also create a shareable link for the uploaded document if required. We can send this link to other recipients by mentioning their email IDs.

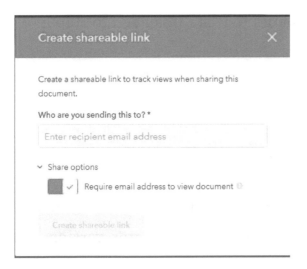

HubSpot can track who has viewed the document that is available on the shareable link when we enable the "Require email address to view document" option.

Insert Document:

We can insert the uploaded document in Emails. We can create new email from the Emails section in the Contact details page. We can click on the Documents link to view the list of documents that we have uploaded in HubSpot.

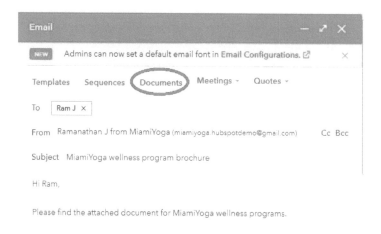

We can click on the Select button for any uploaded document to insert the link for the same in Email. Email recipient can then click on this link to view the document.

Following screenshot displays the Insert document page.

The compose email page will now include the link for uploaded document.

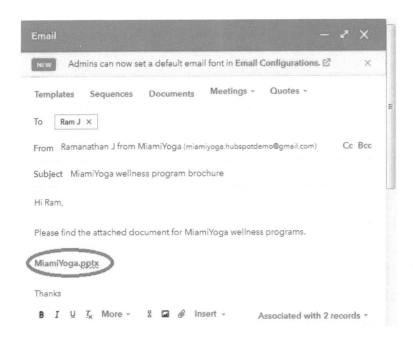

The Document details page will now include updated metrics regarding number of links created, number of visitors and views.

We can click on the link for any visitor to view the detailed metrics such as time spent in seconds on each page of the document that was shared with the recipient.

The Activity section within the Contact detail page also displays when the Contact viewed the shared content.

Hence, we can observe user response for a document by providing a shareable link for this document after uploading the same to HubSpot. We can subscribe for Sales Hub Starter version in case if we want to upload more than five documents.

SALES HUB – MEETINGS

One of the key aspects of interaction with customers or prospects is to assign time for meetings. These meetings could serve various purposes such as to understand customer requirements, to present details about products or services to prospects or to engage in pricing negotiations. Business owners often need to communicate repeatedly with customers or prospects in order to fix time for meetings.

You can activate Meetings application within HubSpot Sales by connecting your Google or Office 365 calendar. You can then enable your prospects or customers to directly book meeting slots on your calendar. You can skip the process of sending multiple emails to your contacts for confirming meeting date and time.

Activating Meetings:

We can the Meetings page from the Sales menu.

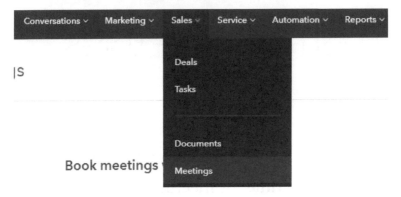

We need to initially connect our Google or Office 365 calendar with HubSpot in order to activate Meetings application. For example, we will connect our Google account for MiamiYoga with HubSpot. We will click on Connect your Google calendar option.

We can review the terms and conditions and then click on Accept and connect to Google button to continue. We cannot use the Google account that we use to connect to HubSpot as a team inbox for meetings as well. Once we connect the appropriate Google account with HubSpot for meetings, we can assign values for various settings such as available times and minimum notice time.

Following screenshot displays the meetings setup page.

We can set a period of rolling weeks or a custom date range in which people can book meeting slots in our calendar.

We can assign form questions that we want to ask our prospects or customers when they are booking meetings on our calendar. We can also choose to either display a default confirmation page or to redirect to another page when a prospect or customer submits a form.

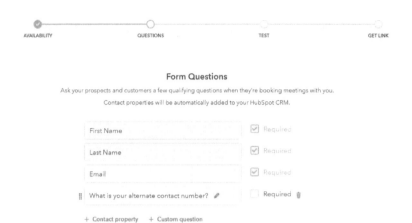

We can then book a test meeting in the next page to see how the Meetings application works.

We can also view the Confirm meeting form page that contains the form fields and questions.

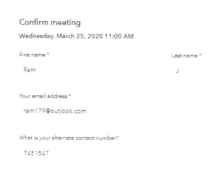

Confirm meeting

Wednesday, March 25, 2020 11:00 AM

First name *

Ram

Last name *

J

Your email address *

ram179@outlook.com

What is your alternate contact number?

7451547

We will receive an email confirmation once we confirm meeting details from the form that is displayed above. We can also get a meeting booking page link that we can share with prospects or customers who can use this link to book meeting time with us.

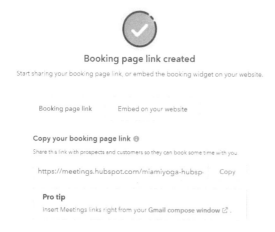

Booking page link created

Start sharing your booking page link, or embed the booking widget on your website.

Booking page link   Embed on your website

Copy your booking page link

Share this link with prospects and customers so they can book some time with you

https://meetings.hubspot.com/miamiyoga-hubsp   Copy

Pro tip

Insert Meetings links right from your Gmail compose window.

119

The Meetings page will now contain the list of meetings that we have created so far.

We can create new personal or team meetings by clicking on the Create meeting link button. We can click on current meeting link to view or edit the details. We can also view the relevant metrics for a meeting such as number of views, meetings booked and conversion rate for a meeting from the Meetings page.

SALES HUB – PLAYBOOKS

Sales teams face a highly competitive environment when they pursue new business in the market. Sales teams need different types of content such as product sheets or pricing guidelines during the course of their discussions with prospects or customers.

Business owners can use the Playbooks application within HubSpot Sales Hub to build sales enablement content for their team. Users can access these playbooks within the HubSpot account itself from contact, deal or company details page. Playbooks application empowers users to store and to access sales collateral from the HubSpot Sales account itself instead of searching for key documents across multiple locations.

A playbook can comprise of call script that lists the relevant questions for a discovery call. A playbook can also include battle card that highlights product or service features. This information can be used by sales teams when presenting to a prospect.

A sales playbook can play a key role in training or onboarding new hires in a sales team. Business users can document product or legacy knowledge with playbooks. New hires can instantly access this knowledge or insight from the corresponding playbooks that are available in HubSpot Sales Hub. Hence, we can use Playbooks application to store sales best practices and resources.

We can access the Playbooks page from the Sales Hub menu as shown in the following image.

Following is the Playbooks page where all the playbooks that we create are listed. We can also organize our playbooks into various folders if required.

Playbooks

New Folder | Create playbook

Build a library of sales best practices and resources.

Build a library of sales best practices and resources. Use rules to auto serve your sales team recommended content, right inside HubSpot.

We can select a type or template when we create a new playbook. We can select the Start from scratch, Call playbook, How-to playbook or Account based selling playbook.

Select a playbook type

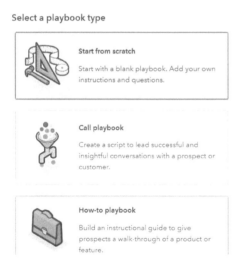

Start from scratch

Start with a blank playbook. Add your own instructions and questions.

Call playbook

Create a script to lead successful and insightful conversations with a prospect or customer.

How-to playbook

Build an instructional guide to give prospects a walk-through of a product or feature.

We will create a playbook from scratch for our case study. We will compile content that sales associates from MiamiYoga can use when they approach individual prospects for new business. We will select the "Start from scratch" option and then click on Create playbook to create a new playbook.

The following image displays the template page for the new playbook where we can edit the content as per our requirements.

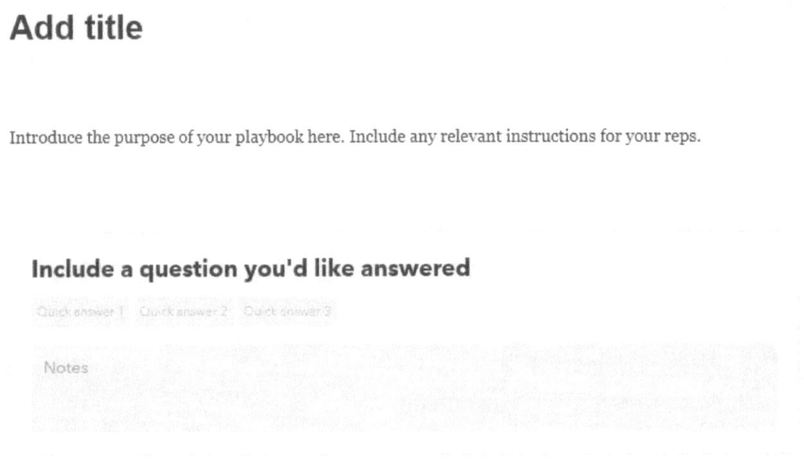

Add title

Introduce the purpose of your playbook here. Include any relevant instructions for your reps.

Include a question you'd like answered

Quick answer 1   Quick answer 2   Quick answer 3

Notes

We will edit the title and enter the purpose for our new playbook.

We can add a question and answer options for our playbook if required. We can click on the Insert question option that is located at the top.

We can view the Create question page when we click on the Insert question option. For example, we will insert a new question that will ask as to for whom the prospect is seeking wellness programs from MiamiYoga. We will use a set of options that will cover the possible responses i.e. for self, for family members or for friends.

We can provide open ended text, set of choices or responses from existing properties in CRM as answer options for our question. We will click on Save to store the question for our playbook.

The playbook will now reflect the updated title, purpose and question.

MiamiYoga Sales Guidance Content

MiamiYoga sales associates can refer to this playbook when they approach individual prospects for selling Yoga based wellness programs.

For whom are you seeking wellness programs

For self   For family members   For friends

Notes

We can include additional questions for our playbook in a similar manner. We can click on Preview link at the top right side of the Playbooks page to view the new playbook. Premium users can publish the playbook if required. We can empower our sales teams by providing relevant content for them through Playbooks in HubSpot. Sales associates can refer to these playbooks that can be designed according to various objectives.

SALES HUB – QUOTES

Speed and efficiency play a crucial role in the sales process. We can ensure a smooth sales process for our prospects by quickly sending them quotes for our products or services. As a result, prospects can refer to the quotes for obtaining pricing related information when they are evaluating the products or services that our business has to offer.

We can create professional looking quotes from the Quotes application in HubSpot Sales Hub. We can insert our company logo and change the colors in quotes to reflect the branding guidelines of our company. We can also assign signers and counter-signers to collect legally binding electronic signatures.

We can streamline quotes-to-cash process by integrating electronic signatures and payment with the Quotes application. We can connect the Quotes application with any Stripe account to collect payment. As a result, a prospect can click to pay through credit card when we send the quote.

Create Quotes:

We can access the Quotes page from the Sales menu.

The Quotes page lists all the quotes created by HubSpot users. We can filter quotes according to the Quote owners or the Quote status value. A Quote status can have various values such as Draft, Pending approval, Signed, Pending payment or Paid.

We can start the quote creation setup wizard by clicking on Create quote in the Quotes page as shown in the following image.

We will now create a quote for our case study. We have earlier created a deal in HubSpot for one of our contacts named Ram J who is interested to know more about the quarterly wellness programs that are offered by MiamiYoga. This prospect has visited the MiamiYoga studio and is currently evaluating as to whether to subscribe to the wellness program. We will now create a quote in HubSpot for this deal record.

The first step in the Quote creation set up wizard comprises of selecting a deal to associate with a quote. In this case, we will select the deal record for the quarterly wellness program that is offered to the prospect Ram J.

Following screenshot displays the Deal association step for creating a quote.

We can click on Next to proceed to the next step for creating a quote. We can select the Quote template as well as provide the Quote name, Quote expiration date and other terms in the Quote Details step of the Quote creation set up wizard.

The quote preview displays the details entered in each step of the Quote creation set up wizard.

We can select the buyer contact information that we want to appear in the quote in the Buyer Information step. In case there are multiple buyers, we can include details of additional contacts in this step. We can also include company details in the Buyer Information step if required.

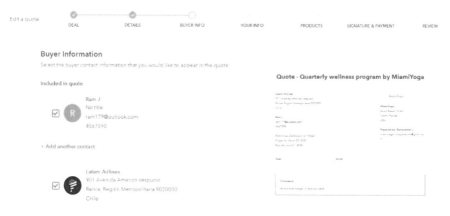

We can click on Next to proceed to the subsequent step for creating a new quote.

We can check our details as well as the information related to our business or company that will appear in the quote in the Your information step of the Quote creation set up wizard.

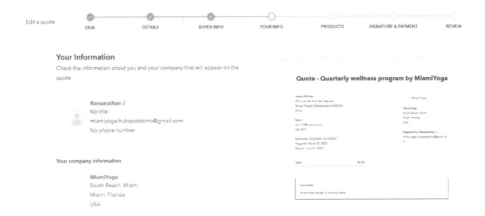

We can include details of the product that is sold by our company to the buyer in the Review Products step.

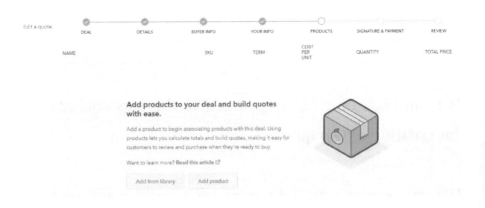

We can directly add product to a quote or we can add a product from the product library. We can access product library from the Product & quotes page for Sales section in Settings.

The following screenshot displays the Products & Quotes page from the Sales section in Settings.

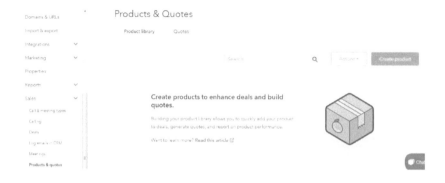

We can click on Create product to add a new product to the product library. We can enter details such as Product name, Description, Price type, Price and Term length in the Create a product page.

We can click on Save to add the product to Product library. We will now click on Add product button in the Review products step to include a product in our quote.

Add product

Product information

Name *

Quarterly Yoga wellness program by MiamiYoga

SKU

3

Description

This is a quarterly Yoga wellness program offered by MiamiYoga

Price   Company currency: US Dollar (USD) $

Price type ⓘ

◉ One-time charge

We can include details such as Product name, SKU, Description, Price type, Price and Term length when we add a product to a quote. The Review Products step will now include the product details as well. We can also include discount, fee or tax related details if required in the Review Products step.

The following screenshot displays the updated Review Products step which now includes product details as well.

We can Save the details and click on Next to proceed to the next step. We can assign the signature and payment options in the subsequent step.

We can either include no signature, use e-signature or we can include space for written signature in our quote. We can also connect a Stripe account in order to bill our prospects directly from our quote. As a result, prospects can pay directly from the quote. We can click on Save to proceed to the Review step.

We can click on Create quote to store the new quote details in HubSpot. A web page for our quote is available when we create the new quote. We can copy the web page link that we can share with prospects. We can also send an email with the quote included.

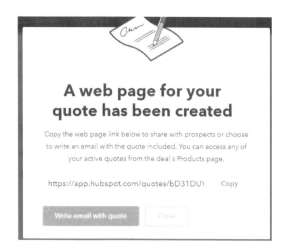

We can include the quote details in the email that we send to a contact by clicking on Quotes menu and selecting the respective quote from the Compose Email page.

The quote related details is now available in the Activity section of the Deals details page.

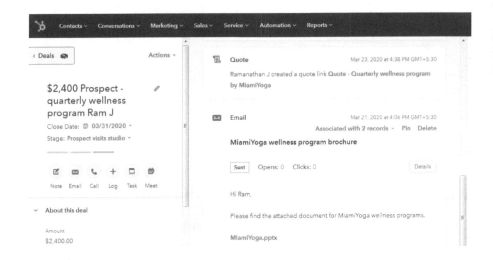

Hence, we can standardize the sales process by sharing professional looking quotes with prospects. Quotes tool in HubSpot provides users with a simple process for creating quotes.

MARKETING HUB – LEAD CAPTURE – FORMS

An average business or company these days have a dedicated website hosted on the internet. Visitors may visit the website for the business through many ways. Some of the users may have searched for a term on Google and then could have accessed the business website from the search results. Other users may have heard of the company from their friends or colleagues, then they would have entered the company name in Google and then these users would have accessed the company website. It is crucial for companies to capture the lead data of visitors who access the company website for various objectives. Business owners should facilitate these visitors to contact the company by providing the necessary tools on their websites.

Lead Capture form application that is available within Marketing Hub in HubSpot enables users to create and to deploy various types of forms. HubSpot users can then share these forms through multiple ways to visitors who might access the business website. HubSpot users can create various types of forms such as Embedded form, Standalone page or pop-up box form that is displayed to website visitors in the corresponding manner.

We can access the Forms page from the Lead Capture section within the Marketing Hub in HubSpot as shown in the following image.

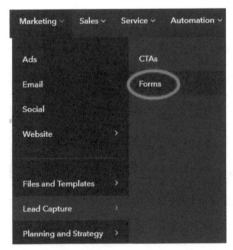

The Forms page lists all forms that a HubSpot user has created so far.

We can click on any form in the Forms page to view more details about the form performance across various metrics. Some of these performance metrics include number of submissions and percentage values across various step completion actions such as Page visits and Interacted with.

We can organize our forms by creating folders within the Forms page. We can create new forms within a folder or we can move the form to an existing folder.

Create Forms:

We can click on Create form button in the Forms page to create a new form. We can then choose the form type in the subsequent step as shown in the following image.

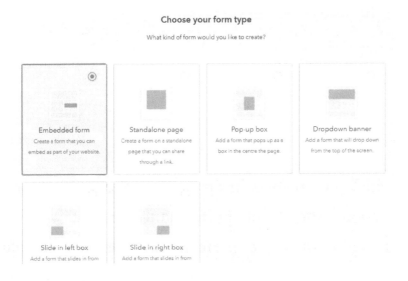

We will choose an embedded form for our example. We will include this embedded form in our MiamiYoga website. This embedded form will be a contact us form which visitors to MiamiYoga website can use to get in touch with the business associates.

We can select the template in the next step for creating a form. There are various types of form templates such as Registration, Contact us and Newsletter signup that we can choose to create a new form. In this case, we will select the Contact us form template.

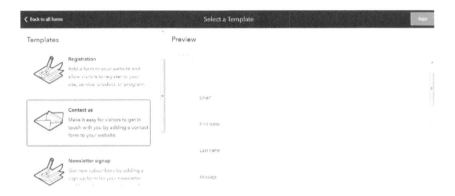

We can observe the form preview in the right side pane of the template selection page. We can now click on the Start button to proceed to the next step.

We can rearrange or include new form fields to our form in this page. For e.g. we will add City and Country Contact properties to our form. We will drag and drop the City and Country property fields from the left pane onto the right side pane.

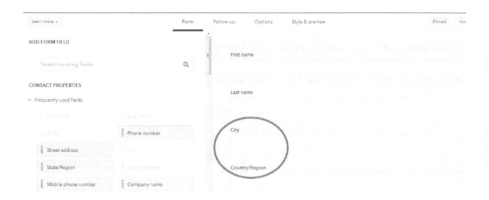

We can rearrange the sequence as per which fields in our form will appear by dragging and dropping the property fields as per our requirement. For e.g. we will place the Email field between the Last name and City fields in our form. We can drag and drop the Email field below the Last name field in our form.

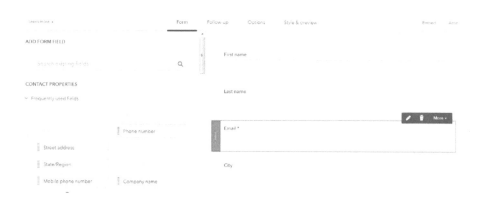

Apart from the property fields that we can drag and drop onto the form, we can also create a new field for our form if required. This new field can be of various types such as single line text, number, drop down and so on. We can also include other elements such as Captcha for Spam prevention in our form. We can also include consent checkboxes and text to our form to follow privacy laws and regulations.

We can view the updated form preview in the right side pane. We can also create a follow up email that we can use to quickly reach out to visitors once they submit the form. We can click on Create follow-up email from the Follow-up section to compose a follow-up email for the visitors who submit details from the Contact us form.

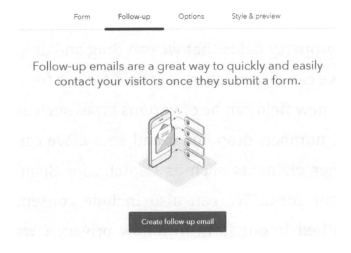

We can select the From user as well as enter the Subject line and email text in the Create email page.

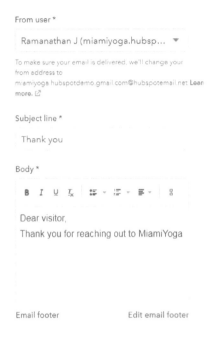

We will need to edit the email footer to enter the relevant details for our follow-up email. We can click on Edit email footer link as shown in the above image to enter details for the email footer.

We can click on Save to store the details for our follow up email. The follow up email will now be visible in the Follow-up section in the Form editing page.

We can add other emails as Follow up emails if required by clicking on Add another email option in the Follow up section for the Form editing page.

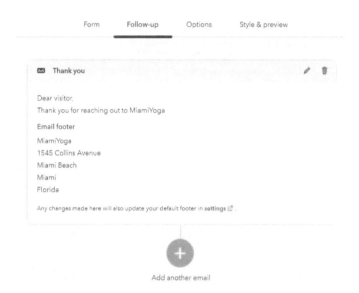

We can set the options for what should happen after a visitor submits a form from the Options section of the Form editing page. We can either display a Thank you message for the visitors or we can redirect them to another page. Similarly, we can also send submission email notifications to the Contact owner if required.

Following screenshot displays the Options section in the Form editing page.

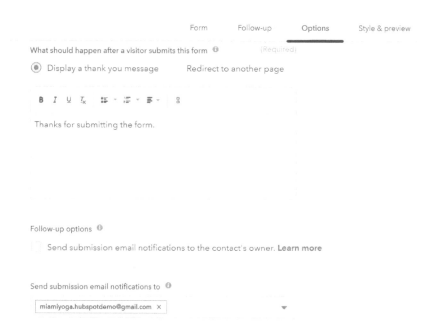

We can assign style settings such as Font, label color, help color and button color from the Style & preview section of the Form editing page. We can also set the theme for the input fields. The theme options include Default, Linear, Sharp or Round values. We can observe the changes that we make to the form in the Preview section on the right side of the page in the Style & preview section.

Following image displays the Style & preview section in the Form editing page.

We can click on the Publish button that is located at the top right side of the Form editing page to publish the latest version of our form.

We will get a form embed code once we publish the form. In case if we have already added a previous version of the form to our website, any updates are automatically applied.

Following image displays the Embed code page.

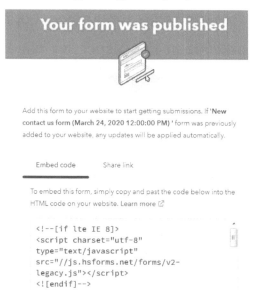

The Forms page will now list the new form that we have created in the previous steps.

We can now embed the Contact us form in the MiamiYoga website using the online editor tool.

Embed Forms:

We can embed HubSpot forms onto the target page of our website by pasting the form code in the respective page. We have hosted the website for our MiamiYoga business on the online website builder tool wix.com.

We will initially install the tracking code for every page of our website just before the </body> tag. We can find the tracking code for HubSpot in the Tracking code link within Reports section in Settings page.

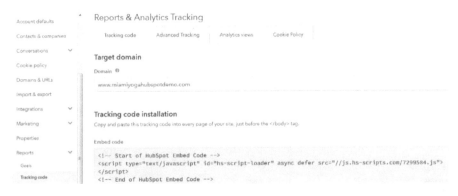

We will now paste this tracking code within every page of our MiamiYoga website. We will open the Tracking and Analytics page within the website editor for Wix.com. We can then insert the code from the Custom option within the New tool menu.

Following screenshot displays the online website editor tool for Wix.com where we have hosted the website for MiamiYoga.

We can insert the tracking code in the subsequent page.

We can now click on Apply to insert the tracking code in all pages of our website.

We will now paste the code in order to insert the HubSpot Embedded form in the About page on the MiamiYoga website. We will place the code for HubSpot form just before the </body> tag.

The Tracking & Analytics page within the website editor tool for Wix.com now displays the tracking codes that we have applied so far.

Following screenshot displays the HubSpot Embedded Form that is now placed in the About page of MiamiYoga website.

We can make any changes as required in the HubSpot embedded form and then click on Publish within the Form editing page in HubSpot. As a result, the updated form will be automatically reflected in the website where we have placed the HubSpot embedded form.

MARKETING HUB – CALLS TO ACTION

The sales process for a business needs intervention by the customer or lead at some stage or point. Business owners might encourage leads to sign up for a newsletter on the website. Other companies might promote an event and as a result they may send an event registration email to current customers. Calls to Action or CTA is an important method for companies to engage customers or leads.

Business owners can use CTAs for various purposes such as on web pages and emails to attract new leads, convert existing leads into customers or to promote an event. CTAs should be action oriented, easily noticeable on a web page or email and visually appealing.

Users can create attractive CTAs in HubSpot. Business owners can place these CTAs across various platforms and then track their performance in HubSpot.

Create CTA:

We can create CTA from the Calls to action page from the Lead Capture section in Marketing Hub.

We can click on the Create CTA button in the Calls to action page to store new CTA in HubSpot.

The Calls to action page stores all the CTAs that users have created in HubSpot.

We will now create a new CTA for our MiamiYoga business. The business owners have decided to start a new monthly newsletter that will describe about the various types of Yoga based exercises. Our new CTA will promote this monthly newsletter and will appeal to visitors to sign up for this newsletter.

We can view the Simple CTA page when we click on Create CTA in the Calls to action page. We can design the CTA button in the initial step of the CTA creation set up.

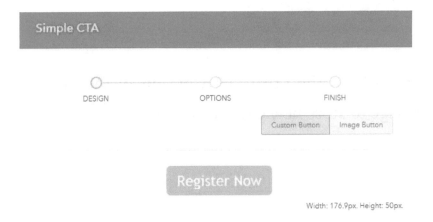

We can assign the button content such as button name, font type and size. We can set the button style according to various options such as Rectangular, Pill or Primary. We can assign the button color as per our requirement. We can also set advanced options for button size and button padding if required. We can either use a custom button or an image button as per our requirement.

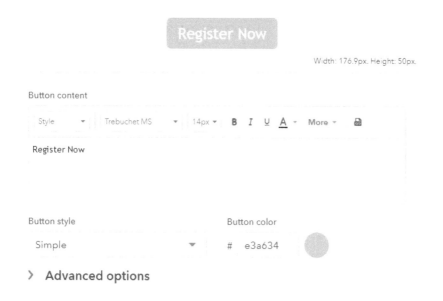

We can click on Next in the Design step in order to proceed to the Options step for creating a CTA.

We can assign an internal name for the CTA in the Options step. We can assign a URL redirect type for our CTA in Options step as well. The URL redirect type can have various values such as Meeting link, External website URL, Email address or File link.

We will select the Email address option for the URL redirect type for our example. We can provide the appropriate email address in the corresponding field. We can also link the CTA to a HubSpot campaign if required.

We can click on Save to complete the Options step. We can now view the CTA.

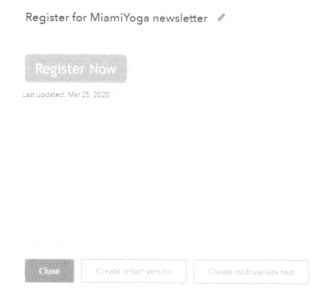

Embed CTA:

We can embed the CTA that we have created in HubSpot onto any web page as required. We can go to the Calls to action page in HubSpot that lists all the CTAs that we have created so far. We can then click on the Actions button for a specific CTA and then click on Embed code option.

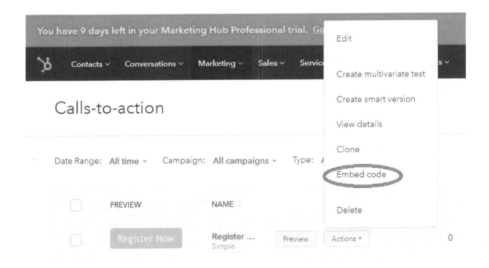

We can copy the embed code from the subsequent page. As we saw earlier with the HubSpot chat bot and embed form, we can insert the code for the CTA in any page of our website as required.

Following image displays the Embed code page for the CTA.

We will install the HubSpot CTA in the Programs page of MiamiYoga website. We will open the Tracking & Analytics page within the online website editor Wix.com to insert the CTA code.

We can click on Custom option within the New Tool menu to insert the HubSpot Embed CTA code. We will place this code just before the </body> tag for the Programs page in the MiamiYoga website.

Following image displays the page for inserting the HubSpot Embed CTA code.

We can click on Apply to insert the HubSpot CTA code in the Programs page for the MiamiYoga website.

We can now observe that the HubSpot CTA code is now applied on the Programs page.

Multivariate CTA:

We can perform multivariate testing by creating various versions of our CTA. We can alter different aspects of our CTA in for different variations. For example, we can enter a different text for button label in one variation of the CTA. Similarly, we can alter the button color in a specific CTA variation.

We can test the response rate for a CTA through multivariate testing. We can create variations of a CTA to test the response rate for each version.

We can access the Calls to action page to view the list of CTAs that we have created so far. We can open the Actions menu for a CTA and click on Create multivariate test option.

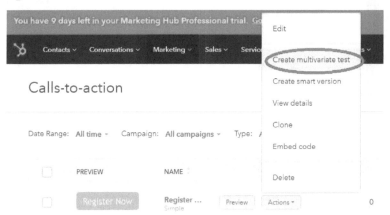

We can create a Variation B for our CTA in the subsequent page. We will use a different button color and label for this variation of the CTA.

We can enter the values for the Options step as per the steps that we followed earlier. We can click on Save to create the Variation B for the CTA.

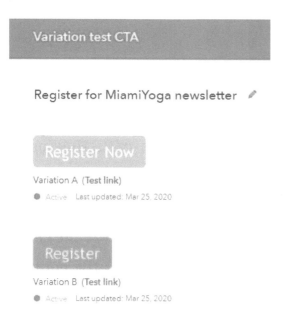

We can create multiple variations of the CTA to assess the performance metrics for each version.

MARKETING HUB – EMAILS

We can engage our active subscribers with HubSpot's email tool. Business owners can send marketing emails to notify subscribers about any news, promotions and offers that might interest them. We can analyze the email campaign results to understand more about the content that is preferred by our contacts.

Marketing email can be one of the most effective tools for business owners to engage with their contacts on a regular basis. Business owners can analyze the performance of their marketing email campaigns across various metrics such as Open rate, Click rate and Click through rate. We can also analyze email performance across other parameters such as low opens and high clicks or low clicks and high opens.

We can access the Marketing Email page from the Marketing menu in HubSpot.

We can manage and analyze marketing email campaigns from the respective tabs in the Marketing Email page. Following image displays the Marketing Email page.

We can filter the Marketing Emails across different criteria such as Draft, Scheduled, Sent and Archived.

Create email:

We will now create a new promotional email for MiamiYoga by clicking on Create email in Marketing email page.

Choose an email type

Regular

Create a beautiful, personalized email and send it to a segment of your contacts.

Automated

Create a personalized, automated email that's sent to contacts when they trigger a workflow

Blog/RSS

With blog or RSS email, you can publish your content once and send updates to your email subscribers.

We will click on the Regular email type to proceed to the next step. We can select a suitable option from the list of email templates that are displayed in the next page. We will select the Promotion email template for our example. We will use the Promotion email template to design an email that will promote MiamiYoga brand and the various wellness programs that are offered by the studio to prospects.

We can edit the email contents in the next step. We can assign a name or title for our promotion email. We can also edit the company logo, images, text and CTA for the promotion email content.

Following screenshot displays the Edit section in the page for creating new email.

The left pane in the Create email page comprises of two sections namely Content and Design. We can add new items such as Image, Text, Button or Social from the Content section in the left pane on to the Email message section on the right side by dragging and dropping the relevant item.

We can also assign the layout for our email message as required by selecting the appropriate layout option. The Design section in the left pane of Create email page comprises of the following options.

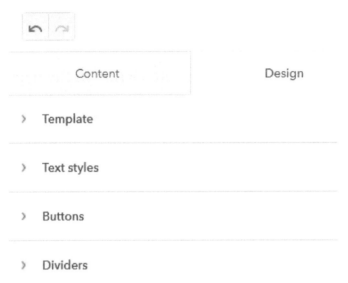

We can assign the background color and pattern from the Template option. Similarly, we can set the paragraph as well as heading font and size from the Text styles option. We can use the Buttons option to set the button radius, color, font type and size. Finally, we can assign Divider properties from the Dividers section.

We can edit each section of our promotion email template by double clicking on the same. For example, we want to insert the MiamiYoga logo at the top of the promotion email. We can double click on the respective section in the email template to edit the content.

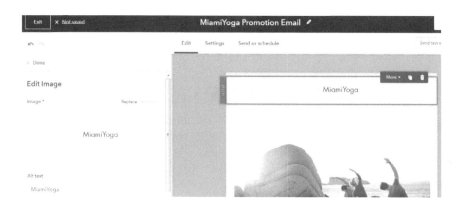

We can click on Replace option in the left pane for editing image and then upload our logo. We can also assign width, height, alignment and alternate text for the MiamiYoga brand image that we have uploaded at the top of the promotional email. We can insert image onto the email template from local drive, URL, Dropbox or Google Drive.

We can similarly edit the content for other sections such as text, button in our promotion email. Following image displays a section of the updated promotion email template for MiamiYoga.

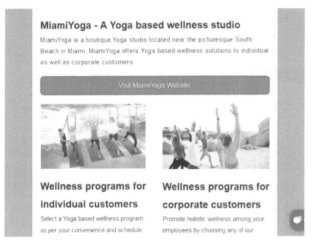

We can now click on the Preview option in the Actions menu to observe as to how our email will appear in Desktop or Mobile screens.

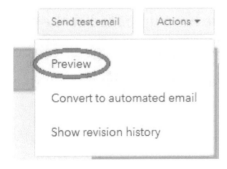

Following screenshot displays the email preview page.

Email Settings:

We can enter details for various fields such as Front name, From address, Subject line in the Settings section for the Create email page.

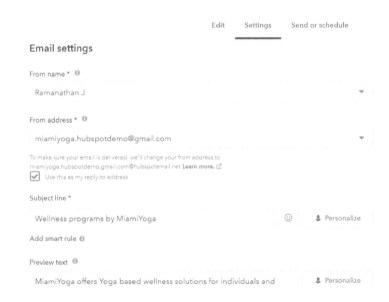

We can also enter details for Internal email name, Subscription type, Campaign and Language in the Settings section as required.

We can also perform A/B test for our marketing emails by clicking on the A/B test switch in the Settings section.

We can alter individual components of our marketing email for each variation in A/B test. For example, we can alter the subject line for each version to analyze the response rate.

When we click on the A/B test switch, we need to enter a name for variation B. In this case, we will use a different subject line for the variation B.

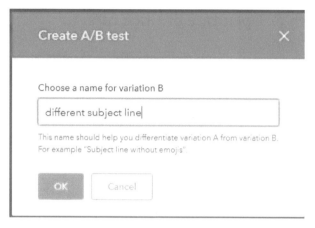

When we click on OK, we can observe the additional options for A/B test. We can now observe two tabs namely Variation A and Variation B. We can edit the settings for each variation by clicking on the respective tab.

Email settings

We will enter a different subject line for Variation A and B. We can assign the test group size for A/B distribution. Similarly, we can also assign test duration and choose the winning metric such as Open rate or Click rate.

Following screenshot displays the settings for A/B distribution.

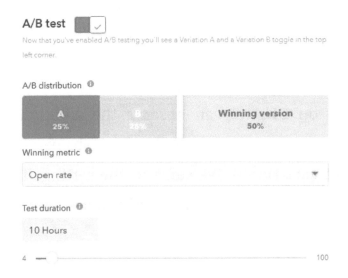

We can select the recipients to whom we want to send the promotion email from the Send or schedule section. We can also select the contacts whom we wish to exclude from receiving the promotion email.

We can send the Marketing email immediately or we can schedule to send the email later. We can accordingly click on the Review and send or Review and schedule option send the marketing email to the recipients.

The Marketing Email page will now display the promotion email that we have sent to the recipients.

We can click on the email link to view detailed performance metrics for the same.

Following screenshot displays a portion of the details page for the MiamiYoga promotion email.

We can also obtain other performance metrics for the marketing email such as top clicked links, top engaged contacts, time spent viewing email or engagement over time from the email details page.

Business owners can utilize email as an effective platform to reach to customers and prospects by constantly analyzing the performance of individual marketing emails and by refining the content to improve engagement with the recipients.

MARKETING HUB – CAMPAIGNS

Marketing efforts in any organization involve a variety of assets and activities at any instant. Many of these marketing efforts are linked to a set of specific goals or objectives for the business. For example, a business can have a goal of adding 20 new customers in a quarter. The business owners can launch various marketing activities in order to achieve this goal. The business owners can send promotion emails, create a new landing page or blog post on their website or send calls to action in this regard.

All the marketing activities and the corresponding assets that are utilized towards achieving a set of specific objectives for a business can be linked to a single campaign.

We can track the performance of our marketing campaigns from the Campaigns page in HubSpot. We can also manage all assets that are required for each campaign from the Campaigns page. We can determine as to which assets in a campaign are engaging contacts and are driving revenue in real time. Finally, we can create goals and measure our campaign performance against these goals.

Create Campaigns:

We can access the Campaigns page from the Planning and Strategy section in Marketing Hub.

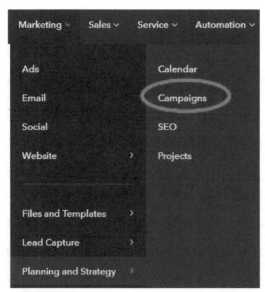

All the marketing campaigns that we create in HubSpot are listed in the Campaigns page. The following screenshot displays the Campaigns page in HubSpot.

We can click on Create campaign in Campaigns page to store the new campaign data. We can assign a campaign name in the subsequent page. For example, we will create a new campaign for promoting MiamiYoga.

We can click on Create to store the campaign data in HubSpot. We will now be redirected to the Campaign details page.

Add Assets:

We can add various types of assets such as blog posts, social posts, calls to action, emails or web pages to a campaign in HubSpot. We can click on the Add assets button in the Campaign details page to include assets to our campaign.

We can choose the specific assets that we want to include in a campaign from the Add assets page.

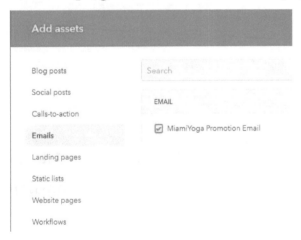

For example, we will include the promotion marketing email and the Calls to action assets that we created earlier for MiamiYoga in our new campaign. We can identify the specific asset in the asset category and then include the same in our HubSpot Campaign by clicking on Save.

The Campaigns details page will now include both assets.

	CTA CLICKS	CTA VIEWS
> Calls-to-action (1)	0	0

	SENT	OPENED	CLICKS
> Emails (1)	1	1	1

Add Budget:

A marketing campaign in any organization will be associated with a budget. This budget amount can be allocated for completing various marketing activities as a part of the campaign. A company can track the overall performance of the marketing campaign by analyzing the allocated budget and the resulting business or revenues after executing the campaign. We can assign the budget for a marketing campaign as per the requirements for creating and assigning individual assets.

We can assign a budget to the marketing campaign in HubSpot by selecting the Edit details option from the Actions menu in Campaign details page.

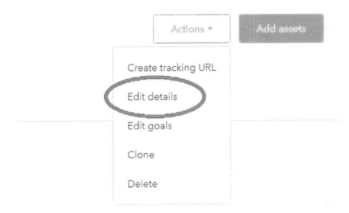

We can assign a budget amount in the subsequent page. We can also mention additional notes for reference if required. We click on Save to assign budget to our campaign.

The Campaigns details page will now mention the budget amount and description.

Add campaign goals:

A marketing campaign in HubSpot comprises of various metrics with which we can evaluate its performance. We can view these metrics from the Campaign details page.

We can view the relevant metrics for a marketing campaign according to the required Date range.

These metrics evaluate a campaign performance from a financial and an engagement level perspectives.

For example, Sessions metric describes the traffic to any web pages, blogs or other landing pages that contain a HubSpot tracking code in a campaign. Hence, when we include these web pages or blog posts as an asset in a marketing campaign, we can derive the traffic numbers for these pages from the Sessions metric.

New contacts metric describe the number of new contacts who interacted with the marketing campaign. The Contact attribution type can have two values namely First touch and Last touch. As a result, New contacts(First touch) metric describes the number of new contacts whose first touch was in a particular marketing campaign. Similarly, New contacts(Last touch) metric describes the number of new contacts whose last touch before becoming a contact was in a specific campaign. New contacts whose first or last touch were outside of a campaign will not be counted in this metric.

Influenced contacts metric show the number of new or existing contacts who engaged with one or more assets in a campaign. For example, an existing contact could have opened a promotional email that is an asset for a marketing campaign.

Closed deals metric indicates the number of deals made by new or influenced contacts. Although the new or influenced contacts could be related to a specific campaign, the deals may not be unique to a campaign.

Influenced revenue metric indicates the total revenue from all closed won deals. Influenced revenue also may not be unique to a campaign.

We can include campaign goals by providing a value for each metric. This goal number will be displayed alongside the metrics in a marketing campaign. We can refer to the business objectives that we seek to achieve from a campaign when we determine the goal values for each metric. Hence, we can set a benchmark for each metric in a marketing campaign by providing a goal value.

We can click on Edit Goals option from the Actions menu in the Campaign Details page to provide a goal value for each metric.

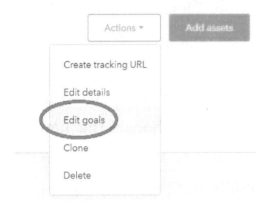

We can assign a value for each metric according to our business objectives or goals.

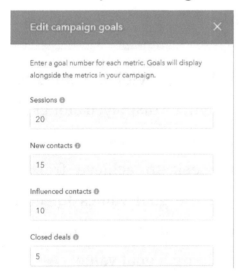

We can click on Save to store the goals for various campaign metrics. The Campaign details page will now display the goal value for each metric.

We can coordinate the marketing efforts in our organization by creating campaigns in HubSpot Marketing Hub. We can assign various types of assets such as marketing emails, blog posts and web pages to a campaign. We can set budget for the overall campaign. We can analyze the performance for each metric in a campaign by allocating a goal value.

Hence, business owners can execute the marketing and brand building strategy for their products or services by creating dedicated campaigns in HubSpot.

SERVICE – TICKETS

One of the key aspects of customer relationship management in any business is to support the customer whenever he/she needs assistance while using the product or service. The extent and quality of customer support that a business provides can determine as to whether the customer continues to purchase a product or service from a company.

A customer usually contacts a business in order to resolve any issue or to address any topic in which he/she needs assistance. The customer can send an email, speak to a customer support executive over phone or chat with a virtual assistant about any aspect of a product or service in which he/she needs guidance.

The quality of customer support in a business depends upon how quickly and effectively the organization is able to address the customer issue. Customers often judge the company or the brand depending upon the quality of their interactions with the support team. As a result, business owners can ensure to provide an appropriate platform for the customer support executives in order to deliver quality customer support.

Companies can use the Tickets page in HubSpot Service to create tickets and assign them to a member of the customer support team. As a result, companies can offer the relevant help at an appropriate time for customers. Companies can use the Tickets page to organize all of the customer inquiries in a single location.

Users can access the Tickets page from the Service menu.

Following screenshot displays the Tickets page.

Create tickets from ticket dashboard:

We can click on Create ticket from the ticket dashboard to store new tickets in HubSpot. For example, we will consider our case study to create a ticket. Let us assume that we have a customer in MiamiYoga who has subscribed for the quarterly wellness program. This customer now wants to upgrade to annual wellness program. As a result, the customer has contacted the customer support team at MiamiYoga over email and has asked for assistance to upgrade to annual wellness program. This requirement of a customer to upgrade to annual wellness program can be addressed by creating a ticket for the same in HubSpot. This ticket can be assigned to a team member at MiamiYoga.

Following screenshot displays a portion of the Create ticket page.

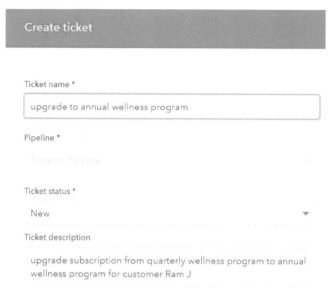

We can provide a ticket name and description as required. We can also assign or edit the Ticket status value according to the current stage of resolution for the ticket. For example, a ticket can have a status value of New if it is logged for the first time by a customer. Similarly, a ticket can have status value of Waiting on contact if the business team is waiting for some input or information from the customer. We will assign the ticket status value as New for our example.

Following screenshots describe the remaining portion of the Create ticket page.

Source value for a ticket indicates the platform from which the customer contacted the business for resolving an issue or a query. In this case, the customer has contacted the business team at MiamiYoga through email and hence we will assign the Source value for this ticket as Email. Other values for Source include Chat, Form and Phone. We can assign a HubSpot or business user as the Ticket owner. This user will be instrumental for addressing the query or issue of a customer and to eventually close the ticket.

We can provide a value of Low, Medium or High for the Priority field in a ticket. We can also assign the ticket creation date to indicate as to when the ticket record was stored in HubSpot.

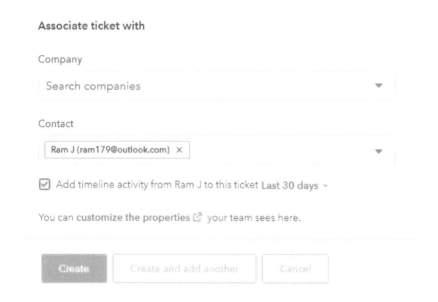

We can associate a ticket to a Company or Contact record depending upon the customer who needs assistance from the company. For example, our current example is related to an individual customer who wants to upgrade to annual wellness program with MiamiYoga. In this case, the ticket will be associated to a Contact record in HubSpot.

On the other hand, if a corporate customer needs assistance from the company, we can associate the relevant ticket for the same to a Company record. We can also add timeline activity such as notes, emails, calls, tasks and meetings from a Contact or Company record to a ticket. This will enable us to associate the interactions between a company and customer with a ticket.

We can click on Create to store the ticket record in HubSpot. The Tickets dashboard will now display the new ticket record.

The default view for Tickets dashboard is in Board format. However, we can also change the dashboard view to Table format if required.

The Tickets dashboard is divided into various columns in which each column indicates a ticket status value. Our new ticket is currently placed in the New column within the Tickets dashboard. We can change the status value for any ticket by dragging and dropping the ticket from one column to another in the Tickets dashboard. For example, suppose the customer support team at MiamiYoga needs payment transaction receipt from the customer before he can be upgraded to annual wellness program. In this case, the ticket status value can be changed to Waiting on Contact.

Following screenshot displays the Tickets dashboard after we drag and drop the ticket from New to Waiting on Contact status value.

We can click on any Ticket record to view the Ticket details page. The Ticket details page is similar to the details page for other properties such as Contacts. The Ticket details page includes individual sections for Activity, Notes, Emails, Calls and Tasks. Once, we drag and drop the ticket from one status value column to another, the Activity section in Ticket details page will display the change in status value.

Following screenshot displays the Ticket details page.

We can change the status value for a ticket from the Ticket details page as well. We can click on the Status menu in the left pane of the Ticket details page to change the Ticket status value.

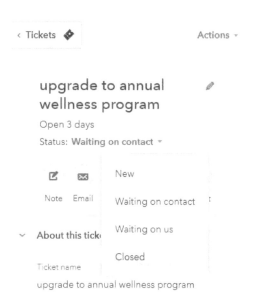

We can click on the field itself or the pencil icon next to each field in the Ticket details page to edit the value of the respective Property.

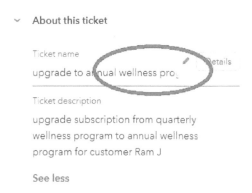

Create Ticket Property:

Some businesses may require additional fields or properties to describe more details about the customer issue or query while creating a ticket. Business users can create a new ticket property in these cases to describe the additional information about a ticket.

Users can click on the View all properties button in the left pane of the Ticket details page to display all the properties related to the Ticket object.

The subsequent page titled Manage properties displays all the properties that will appear when we view the information about a ticket.

We can either make changes to properties that will be visible only to us or we can set the default properties for all users.

For example, suppose we want to know the current subscription of a customer for MiamiYoga when we create a ticket. We can create a new property called Program type that will indicate the wellness program that a customer has currently subscribed to. Program type can have values of Monthly, Quarterly, Half-yearly or Annual.

We can click on Create a ticket property in the Manage properties page to add a new property for the Ticket object.

We can then click on Create property in the Settings page to add a new property.

We can provide details about the new property such as the Object type, Group, Label and Description in the Create a new property page. Object type indicates the object for which we are creating a new property.

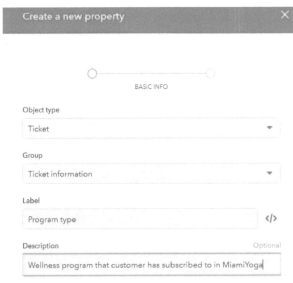

We can click on Next to proceed to the subsequent step for creating a new property.

We can assign the field type for our new property in the next step. In this case, we will choose dropdown list as the field type for the Program type property. We can provide the label values for the field type.

We can view how the new property and its values will appear from the Preview section. We can click on Create to store the new property for the ticket object.

We can click on View all properties button from the Ticket details page to view the Manage properties page for the Ticket object.

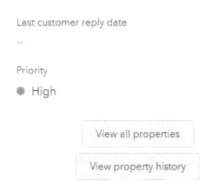

The Manage properties page will now display the new property titled Program type.

When we click on Add to your view, the property will be visible for users in the Ticket details page.

Following screenshot displays the Ticket details page that now displays the new property as well.

Create ticket from Contacts page:

We can also create a ticket for a contact from the Contacts page. We can access the Contacts page as shown in the following image.

We can click on the Preview button against a contact record to open the Contact preview pane.

We can click on the Add ticket link within the Tickets section in the Contact preview pane to add a new ticket for the Contact.

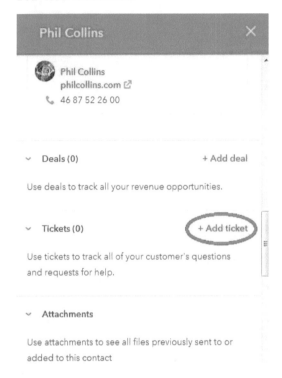

We can either create a new ticket or we can add existing ticket from the Add tickets to this contact page. We can provide details such as Ticket name, Status, Description and Source when we create a new ticket for a contact. We can click on the Add existing ticket tab to search for existing tickets and to add the same to a contact.

Following screenshot displays the Add tickets to this contact page.

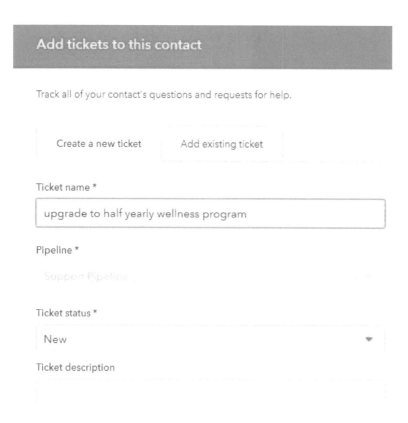

Business owners can track and close customer service requests by utilizing the Tickets application in HubSpot. Users can utilize Tickets application to standardize the process of providing customer support.

AUTOMATION – WORKFLOWS

Business owners can automate marketing and sales related processes in their organizations by utilizing the Workflows application in HubSpot. Companies can create workflows that can be executed depending upon the respective trigger conditions. Similarly, the type of activities that are completed through workflows can range from sending an email to creating a task for a contact.

Workflows application in HubSpot can be utilized for various types of objects such as Contact, Deal, Company and Quotes. Users can analyze the processes related to each of these objects before determining the activities that can be automated. Business owners can improve efficiency of various processes through workflows.

Create Workflows:

We can access the Workflows page from the Automation menu.

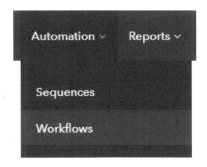

All the workflows that we create in HubSpot are listed in the Workflows page.

We can filter the workflows that are listed in the Workflows page according to various criteria such as the type of workflows, users who have created a workflow and the workflow status value.

We can click on Create workflow to store a new workflow in HubSpot.

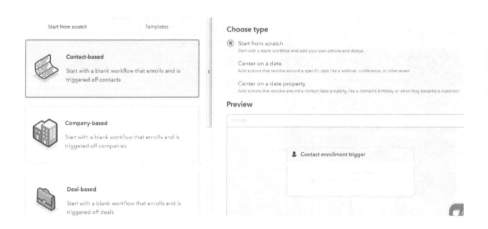

We can create a blank workflow that enrolls and is triggered off Contacts, Companies, Deals, Tickets or Quotes. We can accordingly choose a workflow type. We will choose the Contact-based workflow and click on Next in order to proceed to the subsequent step.

We can add various steps in the Workflow creation page as per our requirements. The initial step in this workflow is called Contact enrollment trigger. We define as to how we want to trigger the contact based automation in the first step.

Following screenshot displays the Workflow creation page.

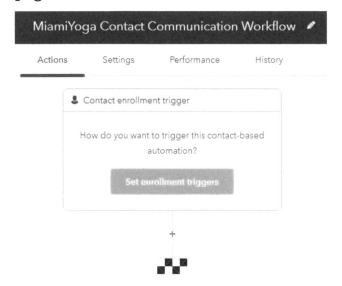

We can click on Set enrollment triggers to define conditions for triggering the workflow. For example, suppose we want to create a workflow that will send an email to contacts and will create a task for contact owner to follow up with the respective contacts. This workflow will be triggered when the Account type value for a Contact is Individual and the Lifecycle stage value is Opportunity. We will set these conditions for enrolling contacts and for triggering the workflow.

Following screenshot displays the Enrollment triggers page.

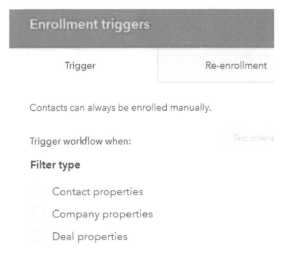

We can click on the Contact properties option for Filter type. Subsequently, we can click on the Account Type field in Contact information section.

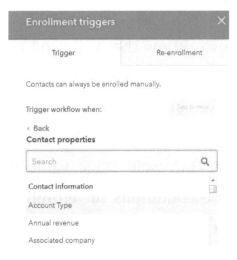

We can select the Individual value for the Account type field.

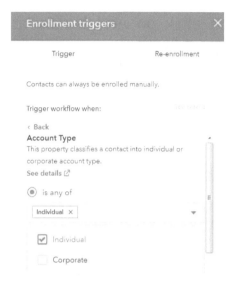

We can click on Apply filter to set this condition for enrollment trigger. We have now defined one condition for triggering the workflow.

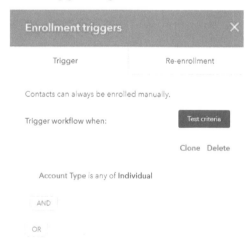

We will now define the second condition for triggering the workflow. As a result, we will set the Lifecycle stage value as Opportunity. We can click on And button as displayed in the previous image to add another condition for triggering the workflow.

We will again choose Contact properties as Filter type and then click on Lifecycle stage property.

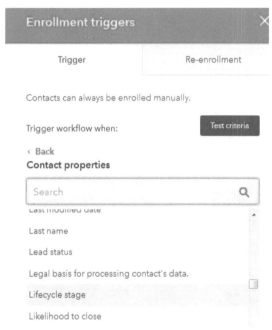

We will select the Lifecycle stage value as Opportunity. We will click on Apply filter to set this condition.

We have now set both conditions for triggering the workflow. We have used the AND logical operator while defining the conditions. Hence, all conditions must be met in order to trigger the workflow. We can also define conditions for triggering the workflow using the OR logical operator.

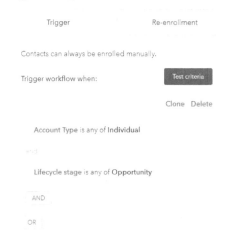

We can click on Save to store the conditions for enrollment trigger. The first step of our workflow is now displayed as follows.

We can click on the plus icon as shown in the above image to add another step to the workflow.

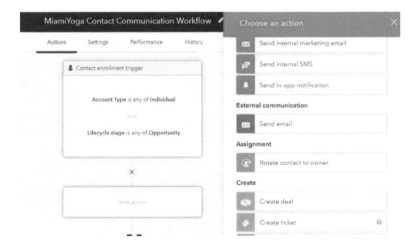

The new step or action can be of various types such as adding a new step in workflow, sending internal or external communication, creating a task and so on. In this case, we will select the Send email option in External communication section. We can select an existing email or we can click on Create new email option to compose the email for external communication.

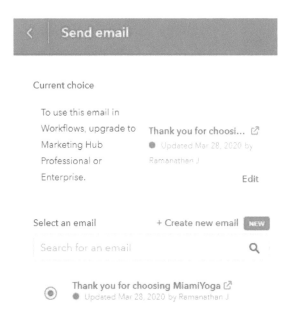

We can enter the details for the email such as Email name, From name, From address and Subject in the Edit email step.

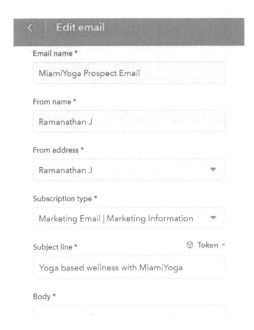

We can click on Save email to store the email details. We can then click on Save to select the email for the next step in the workflow.

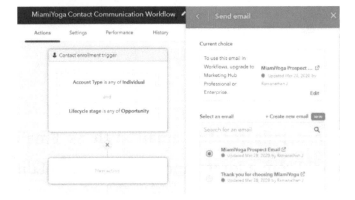

Following image displays the updated workflow.

We can click on the plus icon to add another step to the workflow. We will now create a task for the contact owner to follow up with the contact in this step of the workflow.

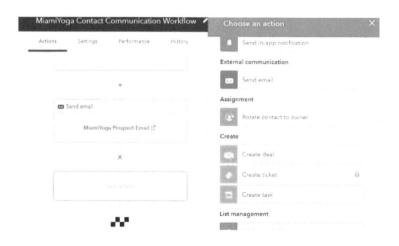

We will click on Create task option within the Create section to add a new task for the workflow. Following image displays the Create task page.

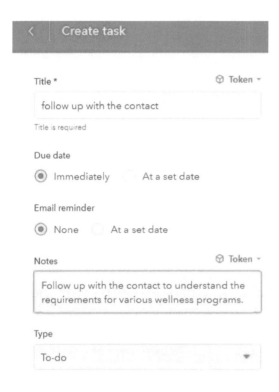

We can click on Save to store the task for the next step in the workflow. We have now completed all the steps for our workflow as per our requirement. We can view all the steps that we have created for our workflow in the Actions section of the Workflows page.

We can determine as to when we want to execute the workflow from the Settings section of the Workflows page. We can also associate a workflow with a campaign from the Settings section.

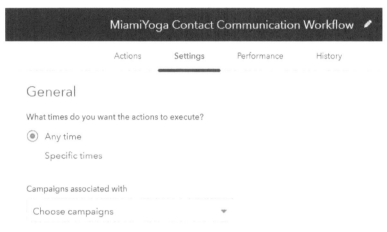

We can view the performance metrics of a workflow from the Performance section of the Workflows page.

We can click on Review at the top of Workflows page to review the workflow settings before we turn on the workflow.

We can edit any of the workflow steps in the subsequent page if required. We can also enroll existing contacts who meet the trigger criteria or we can enroll only those contacts who meet the trigger criteria after we turn on the workflow.

We can click on the Turn on button to turn on the workflow. The Workflows page will now contain the new workflow.

We will now create a new contact record from the Contacts page. We will initially set the Account type value for this contact as Individual. We will also set the Lifecycle stage value for this contact as Subscriber. Following image displays the Contact details page for the new contact.

We will now test the workflow that we created earlier by changing the Lifecycle stage value for our new contact from Subscriber to Opportunity.

Our new contact now has an Account Type value of Individual and the Lifecycle stage value as Opportunity. As a result, both the conditions for triggering the workflow are satisfied. The workflow will now be triggered. As a result, the tasks that are defined in the workflow for sending an email to the contact and for creating a task for the contact owner to follow up with the contact will now be completed.

We can now check the Tasks section in the Contact Details page.

We can observe that the follow up task as defined in the workflow step is now available for the contact. Hence, Workflows application in HubSpot provide an effective platform for business owners to automate the marketing or sales processes in their organizations.

CONCLUSION

We have now looked at a wide variety of capabilities that HubSpot offers as a growth platform to customers. HubSpot CRM enables customers to store details about various objects such as contacts, companies and deals. Customers can simplify email conversations by utilizing the Conversations application.

Business owners can track deals that are happening with various prospects through the Deals application in HubSpot Sales Hub. We can document best practices for Sales teams through Playbooks and create professional looking quote documents through Quotes. CTAs and Forms applications in HubSpot Marketing Hub enable companies to capture lead data from various sources such as websites.

Business owners can utilize the Campaigns application within HubSpot Marketing Hub to define goals, to set budget and to assign various assets such as Emails and Blog posts for a marketing campaign. Companies can use the Tickets application in HubSpot Service Hub to provide effective customer support.

Customers can try the various features that are available in the free HubSpot CRM product as per their business requirements. Customers can start with simple activities such as storing lead and customer data in HubSpot CRM. Customers can also try to capture conversations or interactions with prospects or customers in the CRM. Customers can then utilize HubSpot CRM to store business development or deals related data.

Hence, business owners can initially aim to explore the complete set of capabilities that are offered by the free HubSpot CRM product. Company owners can then check the extent to which they have been able to scale their business by using HubSpot CRM.

If the company owners later determine that they need to use the premium features that are available in the various products of HubSpot growth platform such as Sales Hub or Marketing Hub in order to further scale their business, then they can purchase the corresponding versions.

I hope that you will use this book as an initial source of reference for exploring the various capabilities that are offered by HubSpot growth platform. You can later rely on your business requirements to utilize the full potential of HubSpot. You can write to me at ramanathanj@outlook.com if you would like to share any idea or insight related to HubSpot. I wish you good luck in your ongoing quest for reaching more customers with HubSpot.

Made in United States
Troutdale, OR
01/30/2024

17298839R00141